when things
fall apart

when things
fall apart

heart advice for
difficult times

pema chödrön

Thorsons
CLASSICS

The Sādhana of Mahamudrā © 1968, 1976 by Chögyam Trungpa,
© 1990 by Diana J. Mukpo. Used by permission of Diana J. Mukpo
and the Nalanda Translation Committee

Thorsons
An imprint of HarperCollins*Publishers*
1 London Bridge Road
London SE1 9GF

www.harpercollins.co.uk

HarperCollins*Publishers*
1st Floor, Watermarque Building, Ringsend Road
Dublin 4, Ireland

First published in the US by Shambhala Publications, Inc. 1997
First published in the UK by Element 2003
This edition published 2017

27

© Pema Chödrön 1997

Pema Chödrön asserts the moral right to
be identified as the author of this work

The author's proceeds from this book will be donated to
Gampo Abbey, Pleasant Bay, Nova Scotia, Canada BOE 2PO

A catalogue record of this book is available from the British Library

ISBN 978-0-00-718351-7

Printed and bound by CPI Group (UK) Ltd, Croydon, CR0 4YY

MIX
Paper from
responsible sources
FSC™ C007454

FSC is a non-profit international organisation established to promote
the responsible management of the world's forests. Products carrying
the FSC label are independently certified to assure consumers that they
come from forests that are managed to meet the social, economic
and ecological needs of present and future generations.

Find out more about HarperCollins and the environment at
www.harpercollins.co.uk/green

To Sakyong Mipham Rinpoche, with
devotion, love and gratitude.

Pema Chödrön is one of the most renowned spiritual teachers in the West today. She is the resident teacher of Buddhism at Gampo Abbey in Cape Breton, Nova Scotia, the first Tibetan monastery in North America. She is the author of four bestselling books, including *The Wisdom of No Escape*, *Start Where You Are* and *The Places that Scare You*.

contents

acknowledgments

My sincere gratitude to Lynne Van de Bunte, who not only preserved the tapes that make up the talks in the book but also spent many hours finding the following people to transcribe them: my thanks to Heidi Utz, Rex Washburn, Ginny Davies, and Aileen and Bill Fell (who also got all the talks on one computer), and also to Lynne herself, who transcribed the tapes that were so ancient, no one else could figure out what was being said. Finally, a very special thank-you to my friend and editor Emily Hilburn Sell, who took a carton of unedited talks and transformed them into this book. Without her talent, hard work, and loving dedication, I would never have published anything. I feel fortunate that we can continue to work together.

introduction

In 1995 I took a sabbatical. For twelve months I essentially did nothing. It was the most spiritually inspiring time of my life. Pretty much all I did was relax. I read and hiked and slept. I cooked and ate, meditated and wrote. I had no schedule, no agenda, and no "shoulds." A lot got digested during this completely open, uncharted time. For one thing, I began to read slowly through two cardboard boxes of very raw, unedited transcriptions of talks I had given from 1987 to 1994. Unlike the dathun talks that make up *The Wisdom of No Escape* and the lojong teachings that make up *Start Where You Are*, these talks seemed to have no unifying thread. Now and then I would look at a few transcripts. I found them everything from pedantic to delightful. It was both interesting and embarrassing to be faced with such a profusion of my own words. Gradually, as I read more, I began to see that in some way, no matter what subject I had chosen, what country I was in, or what year it was, I had taught endlessly about the same things: the great need for *maitri* (loving-kindness toward oneself), and developing from that the awakening of a fearlessly compassionate attitude toward our own pain and that of others. It seemed to me that the view behind every single talk was that we could step into uncharted territory and relax with the groundlessness of our situation. The other underlying theme was dissolving the dualistic tension between us and them, this and that,

1

good and bad, by inviting in what we usually avoid. My teacher, Chögyam Trungpa Rinpoche, described this as "leaning into the sharp points." It occurred to me that for all those seven years, I'd been simply trying to digest and communicate the helpful and very gutsy instructions that Trungpa Rinpoche gave his students.

As I delved into the boxes, I could see that I still had a long way to go before fully appreciating what I had been taught. I also saw that by putting Rinpoche's advice into practice as well as I could, and by attempting to share this experience of a student's path with others, I had found a kind of fundamental happiness and contentment that I'd never known before. It made me laugh to see that, just as I had so often said, making friends with our own demons and their accompanying insecurity leads to a very simple, understated relaxation and joy.

About halfway through the year, my editor, Emily Hilburn Sell, happened to ask me if I had any more talks that might be usable for a third book. I sent her the cardboard boxes. She read through the transcripts and felt inspired to tell Shambhala Publications, "We have another book."

Over the next six months, Emily sifted and shifted and deleted and edited, and I had the luxury to work further on each chapter to my heart's content. When I wasn't resting or looking at the ocean or walking in the hills, I would get totally absorbed by these talks. Rinpoche once gave me the advice "Relax and write." At the time it didn't seem like I'd ever do either of these things, but years later, here

I was following his instructions.

The result of this collaboration with Emily and my year of doing nothing is this book.

May it encourage you to settle down with your life and take these teachings on honesty, kindness, and bravery to heart. If your life is chaotic and stressful, there's plenty of advice here for you. If you're in transition, suffering from loss, or just fundamentally restless, these teachings are tailor made. The main point is that we all need to be reminded and encouraged to relax with whatever arises and bring whatever we encounter to the path.

In putting these instructions into practice, we join a long lineage of teachers and students who have made the buddha dharma relevant to the ups and downs of their ordinary lives.

Just as they made friends with their egos and discovered wisdom mind, so can we.

I thank the Vidyadhara, the Venerable Chögyam Trungpa Rinpoche, for totally committing his life to the dharma and for being so eager to transmit its essence to the people of the West. May the inspiration I received from him be contagious.

May we, like him, lead the life of a bodhisattva, and may we not forget his proclamation that "Chaos should be regarded as extremely good news."

PEMA CHÖDRÖN
Gampo Abbey
Pleasant Bay, Nova Scotia, 1996

one

intimacy with fear

*Fear is a natural reaction to moving
closer to the truth.*

Embarking on the spiritual journey is like getting
into a very small boat and setting out on the ocean
to search for unknown lands. With wholehearted
practice comes inspiration, but sooner or later we will
also encounter fear. For all we know, when we get to the
horizon, we are going to drop off the edge of the world.
Like all explorers, we are drawn to discover what's waiting
out there without knowing yet if we have the courage to
face it.

If we become interested in Buddhism and decide to
find out what it has to offer, we'll soon discover that there
are different slants on how we can proceed. With insight
meditation we begin practicing mindfulness, being fully
present with all our activities and thoughts. With Zen
practice we hear teachings on emptiness and are challenged to connect with the open, unbounded clarity of
mind. The vajrayana teachings introduce us to the notion
of working with the energy of all situations, seeing whatever arises as inseparable from the awakened state. Any of
these approaches might hook us and fuel our enthusiasm

to explore further, but if we want to go beneath the surface and practice without hesitation, it is inevitable that at some point we will experience fear.

Fear is a universal experience. Even the smallest insect feels it. We wade in the tidal pools and put our finger near the soft open bodies of sea anemones and they close up. Everything spontaneously does that. It's not a terrible thing that we feel fear when faced with the unknown. It is part of being alive, something we all share. We react against the possibility of loneliness, of death, of not having anything to hold on to. Fear is a natural reaction to moving closer to the truth.

If we commit ourselves to staying right where we are, then our experience becomes very vivid. Things become very clear when there is nowhere to escape.

During a long retreat, I had what seemed to me the earth-shaking revelation that we cannot be in the present and run our story lines at the same time! It sounds pretty obvious, I know, but when you discover something like this for yourself, it changes you. Impermanence becomes vivid in the present moment; so do compassion and wonder and courage. And so does fear. In fact, anyone who stands on the edge of the unknown, fully in the present without reference point, experiences groundlessness. That's when our understanding goes deeper, when we find that the present moment is a pretty vulnerable place and that this can be completely unnerving and completely tender at the same time.

When we begin our exploration, we have all kinds of

ideals and expectations. We are looking for answers that will satisfy a hunger we've felt for a very long time. But the last thing we want is a further introduction to the boogey-man. Of course, people do try to warn us. I remember when I first received meditation instruction, the woman told me the technique and guidelines on how to practice and then said, "But please don't go away from here think-ing that meditation is a vacation from irritation." Some-how all the warnings in the world don't quite convince us. In fact they draw us closer.

What we're talking about is getting to know fear, becoming familiar with fear, looking it right in the eye— not as a way to solve problems, but as a complete undoing of old ways of seeing, hearing, smelling, tasting, and thinking. The truth is that when we really begin to do this, we're going to be continually humbled. There's not going to be much room for the arrogance that holding on to ideals can bring. The arrogance that inevitably does arise is going to be continually shot down by our own courage to step forward a little further. The kinds of discoveries that are made through practice have nothing to do with believing in anything. They have much more to do with having the courage to die, the courage to die continually.

Instructions on mindfulness or emptiness or working with energy all point to the same thing: being right on the spot nails us. It nails us right to the point of time and space that we are in. When we stop there and don't act out, don't repress, don't blame it on anyone else, and also don't blame it on ourselves, then we meet with an open-ended question that has no conceptual answer. We also encounter our heart. As one student so eloquently put it, "Buddha nature, cleverly disguised as fear, kicks our ass into being receptive."

I once attended a lecture about a man's spiritual experiences in India in the 1960s. He said he was determined to get rid of his negative emotions. He struggled against anger and lust; he struggled against laziness and pride. But mostly he wanted to get rid of his fear. His meditation teacher kept telling him to stop struggling, but he took that as just another way of explaining how to overcome his obstacles.

Finally the teacher sent him off to meditate in a tiny hut in the foothills. He shut the door and settled down to practice, and when it got dark he lit three small candles. Around midnight he heard a noise in the corner of the room, and in the darkness he saw a very large snake. It looked to him like a king cobra. It was right in front of him, swaying. All night he stayed totally alert, keeping his eyes on the snake. He was so afraid that he couldn't move. There was just the snake and himself and fear.

Just before dawn the last candle went out, and he began to cry. He cried not in despair but from tenderness. He felt the longing of all the animals and people in the world; he knew their alienation and their struggle. All his meditation had been nothing but further separation and struggle. He accepted—really accepted wholeheartedly—that he was angry and jealous, that he resisted and struggled, and that he was afraid. He accepted that he was also precious beyond measure—wise and foolish, rich and poor, and totally unfathomable. He felt so much gratitude that in the total darkness he stood up, walked toward the snake, and bowed. Then he fell sound asleep on the floor. When he awoke, the snake was gone. He never knew if it was his imagination or if it had really been there, and it didn't seem to matter. As he put it at the end of the lecture, that much intimacy with fear caused his dramas to collapse, and the world around him finally got through.

No one ever tells us to stop running away from fear. We are very rarely told to move closer, to just be there, to become familiar with fear. I once asked the Zen master Kobun Chino Roshi how he related with fear, and he said, "I agree. I agree." But the advice we usually get is to sweeten it up, smooth it over, take a pill, or distract ourselves, but by all means make it go away.

We don't need that kind of encouragement, because dissociating from fear is what we do naturally. We habitually spin off and freak out when there's even the merest hint of fear. We feel it coming and we check out. It's good to know we do that—not as a way to beat ourselves up, but as a way to develop unconditional compassion. The most heartbreaking thing of all is how we cheat ourselves of the present moment.

Sometimes, however, we are cornered; everything falls apart, and we run out of options for escape. At times like that, the most profound spiritual truths seem pretty straightforward and ordinary. There's nowhere to hide. We see it as well as anyone else—*better* than anyone else. Sooner or later we understand that although we can't make fear look pretty, it will nevertheless introduce us to all the teaching we've ever heard or read.

So the next time you encounter fear, consider yourself lucky. This is where the courage comes in. Usually we think that brave people have no fear. The truth is that they are intimate with fear. When I was first married, my husband said I was one of the bravest people he knew. When I asked him why, he said because I was a complete coward but went ahead and did things anyhow.

The trick is to keep exploring and not bail out, even when we find out that something is not what we thought. That's what we're going to discover again and again and again. Nothing is what we thought. I can say that with great confidence. Emptiness is not what we thought. Neither is mindfulness or fear. Compassion—not what we thought. Love. Buddha nature. Courage. These are code words for things we don't know in our minds, but any of us could experience them. These are words that point to what life really is when we let things fall apart and let ourselves be nailed to the present moment.

two

when things fall apart

When things fall apart and we're on the verge of we know
not what, the test of each of us is to stay on that brink and
not concretize. The spiritual journey is not about heaven
and finally getting to a place that's really swell.

Gampo Abbey is a vast place where the sea and the
sky melt into each other. The horizon extends
infinitely, and in this vast space float seagulls and
ravens. The setting is like a huge mirror that exaggerates
the sense of there being nowhere to hide. Also, since it is
a monastery, there are very few means of escape—no
lying, no stealing, no alcohol, no sex, no exit.

Gampo Abbey was a place to which I had been longing
to go. Trungpa Rinpoche asked me to be the director of
the abbey, so finally I found myself there. Being there was
an invitation to test my love of a good challenge, because
in the first years it was like being boiled alive.

What happened to me when I got to the abbey was
that everything fell apart. All the ways I shield myself, all
the ways I delude myself, all the ways I maintain my
well-polished self-image—all of it fell apart. No matter

how hard I tried, I couldn't manipulate the situation. My style was driving everyone else crazy, and I couldn't find anywhere to hide.

I had always thought of myself as a flexible, obliging person who was well liked by almost everyone. I'd been able to carry this illusion throughout most of my life. During my early years at the abbey, I discovered that I had been living in some kind of misunderstanding. It wasn't that I didn't have good qualities, it was just that I was not the ultimate golden girl. I had so much invested in that image of myself, and it just wasn't holding together anymore. All my unfinished business was exposed vividly and accurately in living Technicolor, not only to myself, but to everyone else as well.

Everything that I had not been able to see about myself before was suddenly dramatized. As if that weren't enough, others were free with their feedback about me and what I was doing. It was so painful that I wondered if I would ever be happy again. I felt that bombs were being dropped on me almost continuously, with self-deceptions exploding all around. In a place where there was so much practice and study going on, I could not get lost in trying to justify myself and blame others. That kind of exit was not available.

A teacher visited during this time, and I remember her saying to me, "When you have made good friends with yourself, your situation will be more friendly too."

I had learned this lesson before, and I knew that it was the only way to go. I used to have a sign pinned up on my

wall that read: "Only to the extent that we expose ourselves over and over to annihilation can that which is
indestructible be found in us." Somehow, even before I
heard the Buddhist teachings, I knew that this was the
spirit of true awakening. It was all about letting go of
everything. Nevertheless, when the bottom falls out and
we can't find anything to grasp, it hurts a lot. It's like the
Naropa Institute motto: "Love of the truth puts you on the
spot." We might have some romantic view of what that
means, but when we are nailed with the truth, we suffer.
We look in the bathroom mirror, and there we are with
our pimples, our aging face, our lack of kindness, our
aggression and timidity—all that stuff.

This is where tenderness comes in. When things are
shaky and nothing is working, we might realize that we
are on the verge of something. We might realize that this
is a very vulnerable and tender place, and that tenderness
can go either way. We can shut down and feel resentful or
we can touch in on that throbbing quality. There is definitely something tender and throbbing about groundlessness.

It's a kind of testing, the kind of testing that spiritual
warriors need in order to awaken their hearts. Sometimes
it's because of illness or death that we find ourselves in
this place. We experience a sense of loss—loss of our
loved ones, loss of our youth, loss of our life.

I have a friend dying of AIDS. Before I was leaving for
a trip, we were talking. He said, "I didn't want this, and I
hated this, and I was terrified of this. But it turns out that

13

this illness has been my greatest gift." He said, "Now every moment is so precious to me. All the people in my life are so precious to me. My whole life means so much to me." Something had really changed, and he felt ready for his death. Something that was horrifying and scary had turned into a gift.

Things falling apart is a kind of testing and also a kind of healing. We think that the point is to pass the test or to overcome the problem, but the truth is that things don't really get solved. They come together and they fall apart. Then they come together again and fall apart again. It's just like that. The healing comes from letting there be room for all of this to happen: room for grief, for relief, for misery, for joy.

When we think that something is going to bring us pleasure, we don't know what's really going to happen. When we think something is going to give us misery, we don't know. Letting there be room for not knowing is the most important thing of all. We try to do what we think is going to help. But we don't know. We never know if we're going to fall flat or sit up tall. When there's a big disappointment, we don't know if that's the end of the story. It may be just the beginning of a great adventure.

I read somewhere about a family who had only one son. They were very poor. This son was extremely precious to them, and the only thing that mattered to his family was that he bring them some financial support and prestige. Then he was thrown from a horse and crippled. It seemed like the end of their lives. Two weeks after that, the army came into the village and took away all the healthy, strong men to fight in the war, and this young man was allowed to stay behind and take care of his family.

Life is like that. We don't know anything. We call something bad; we call it good. But really we just don't know.

When things fall apart and we're on the verge of we know not what, the test for each of us is to stay on that brink and not concretize. The spiritual journey is not about heaven and finally getting to a place that's really swell. In fact, that way of looking at things is what keeps us miserable. Thinking that we can find some lasting pleasure and avoid pain is what in Buddhism is called samsara, a hopeless cycle that goes round and round endlessly and causes us to suffer greatly. The very first noble truth of the Buddha points out that suffering is inevitable for human beings as long as we believe that things last—that they don't disintegrate, that they can be counted on to satisfy our hunger for security. From this point of view, the only time we ever know what's really going on is when the rug's been pulled out and we can't find anywhere to land. We use these situations either to wake ourselves up or to put ourselves to sleep. Right now—in the very instant of groundlessness—is the seed of taking care of those who need our care and of discovering our goodness.

I remember so vividly a day in early spring when my whole reality gave out on me. Although it was before I had heard any Buddhist teachings, it was what some would call a genuine spiritual experience. It happened when my husband told me he was having an affair. We lived in northern New Mexico. I was standing in front of our adobe house drinking a cup of tea. I heard the car drive up and the door bang shut. Then he walked around the corner, and without warning he told me that he was having an affair and he wanted a divorce.

I remember the sky and how huge it was. I remember the sound of the river and the steam rising up from my tea. There was no time, no thought, there was nothing—just the light and a profound, limitless stillness. Then I regrouped and picked up a stone and threw it at him.

When anyone asks me how I got involved in Buddhism, I always say it was because I was so angry with my husband. The truth is that he saved my life. When that marriage fell apart, I tried hard—very, very hard—to go back to some kind of comfort, some kind of security, some kind of familiar resting place. Fortunately for me, I could never pull it off. Instinctively I knew that annihilation of my old dependent, clinging self was the only way to go. That's when I pinned that sign up on my wall.

Life is a good teacher and a good friend. Things are always in transition, if we could only realize it. Nothing ever sums itself up in the way that we like to dream about. The off-center, in-between state is an ideal situation, a situation in which we don't get caught and we can open our hearts and minds beyond limit. It's a very tender, nonaggressive, open-ended state of affairs.

To stay with that shakiness—to stay with a broken

heart, with a rumbling stomach, with the feeling of hopelessness and wanting to get revenge—that is the path of true awakening. Sticking with that uncertainty, getting the knack of relaxing in the midst of chaos, learning not to panic—this is the spiritual path. Getting the knack of catching ourselves, of gently and compassionately catching ourselves, is the path of the warrior. We catch ourselves one zillion times as once again, whether we like it or not, we harden into resentment, bitterness, righteous indignation—harden in any way, even into a sense of relief, a sense of inspiration.

Every day we could think about the aggression in the world, in New York, Los Angeles, Halifax, Taiwan, Beirut, Kuwait, Somalia, Iraq, everywhere. All over the world, everybody always strikes out at the enemy, and the pain escalates forever. Every day we could reflect on this and ask ourselves, "Am I going to add to the aggression in the world?" Every day, at the moment when things get edgy, we can just ask ourselves, "Am I going to practice peace, or am I going to war?"

three

this very moment is the perfect teacher

We can meet our match with a poodle or with a raging guard dog, but the interesting question is—what happens next?

Generally speaking, we regard discomfort in any form as bad news. But for practitioners or spiritual warriors—people who have a certain hunger to know what is true—feelings like disappointment, embarrassment, irritation, resentment, anger, jealousy, and fear, instead of being bad news, are actually very clear moments that teach us where it is that we're holding back. They teach us to perk up and lean in when we feel we'd rather collapse and back away. They're like messengers that show us, with terrifying clarity, exactly where we're stuck. This very moment is the perfect teacher, and, lucky for us, it's with us wherever we are.

Those events and people in our lives who trigger our unresolved issues could be regarded as good news. We don't have to go hunting for anything. We don't need to try to create situations in which we reach our limit. They occur all by themselves, with clockwork regularity.

Each day, we're given many opportunities to open up or shut down. The most precious opportunity presents itself when we come to the place where we think we can't handle whatever is happening. It's too much. It's gone too far. We feel bad about ourselves. There's no way we can manipulate the situation to make ourselves come out looking good. No matter how hard we try, it just won't work. Basically, life has just nailed us.

It's as if you just looked at yourself in the mirror, and you saw a gorilla. The mirror's there; it's showing you, and what you see looks bad. You try to angle the mirror so you will look a little better, but no matter what you do, you still look like a gorilla. That's being nailed by life, the place where you have no choice except to embrace what's happening or push it away.

Most of us do not take these situations as teachings. We automatically hate them. We run like crazy. We use all kinds of ways to escape—all addictions stem from this moment when we meet our edge and we just can't stand it. We feel we have to soften it, pad it with something, and we become addicted to whatever it is that seems to ease the pain. In fact, the rampant materialism that we see in the world stems from this moment. There are so many ways that have been dreamt up to entertain us away from the moment, soften its hard edge, deaden it so we don't have to feel the full impact of the pain that arises when we cannot manipulate the situation to make us come out looking fine.

Meditation is an invitation to notice when we reach our limit and to not get carried away by hope and fear. Through meditation, we're able to see clearly what's going on with our thoughts and emotions, and we can also let them go. What's encouraging about meditation is that even if we shut down, we can no longer shut down in ignorance. We see very clearly that we're closing off. That in itself begins to illuminate the darkness of ignorance. We're able to see how we run and hide and keep ourselves busy so that we never have to let our hearts be penetrated. And we're also able to see how we could open and relax.

Basically, disappointment, embarrassment, and all these places where we just cannot feel good are a sort of death. We've just lost our ground completely; we are unable to hold it together and feel that we're on top of things. Rather than realizing that it takes death for there to be birth, we just fight against the fear of death.

Reaching our limit is not some kind of punishment. It's actually a sign of health that, when we meet the place where we are about to die, we feel fear and trembling. A further sign of health is that we don't become undone by fear and trembling, but we take it as a message that it's time to stop struggling and look directly at what's threatening us. Things like disappointment and anxiety are messengers telling us that we're about to go into unknown territory.

Our bedroom closet can be unknown territory for some of us. For others, it's going into outer space. What evokes hope and fear for me is different from what brings

21

it up for you. My aunt reaches her limit when I move a lamp in her living room. My friend completely loses it when she has to move to a new apartment. My neighbor is afraid of heights. It doesn't really matter what causes us to reach our limit. The point is that sooner or later it happens to all of us.

The first time I met Trungpa Rinpoche was with a class of fourth graders who asked him a lot of questions about growing up in Tibet and about escaping from the Chinese Communists into India. One boy asked him if he was ever afraid. Rinpoche answered that his teacher had encouraged him to go to places like graveyards that scared him and to experiment with approaching things he didn't like. Then he told a story about traveling with his attendants to a monastery he'd never seen before. As they neared the gates, he saw a large guard dog with huge teeth and red eyes. It was growling ferociously and struggling to get free from the chain that held it. The dog seemed desperate to attack them. As Rinpoche got closer, he could see its bluish tongue and spittle spraying from its mouth. They walked past the dog, keeping their distance, and entered the gate. Suddenly the chain broke and the dog rushed at them. The attendants screamed and froze in terror. Rinpoche turned and ran as fast as he could— straight at the dog. The dog was so surprised that he put his tail between his legs and ran away.

We can meet our match with a poodle or with a raging guard dog, but the interesting question is—what happens next?

The spiritual journey involves going beyond hope and fear, stepping into unknown territory, continually moving forward. The most important aspect of being on the spiritual path may be to just keep moving. Usually, when we reach our limit, we feel exactly like Rinpoche's attendants and freeze in terror. Our bodies freeze and so do our minds.

How do we work with our minds when we meet our match? Rather than indulge or reject our experience, we can somehow let the energy of the emotion, the quality of what we're feeling, pierce us to the heart. This is easier said than done, but it's a noble way to live. It's definitely the path of compassion—the path of cultivating human bravery and kindheartedness.

In the teachings of Buddhism, we hear about egolessness. It sounds difficult to grasp: what are they talking about, anyway? When the teachings are about neurosis, however, we feel right at home. That's something we really understand. But egolessness? When we reach our limit, if we aspire to know that place fully—which is to say that we aspire to neither indulge nor repress—a hardness in us will dissolve. We will be softened by the sheer force of whatever energy arises—the energy of anger, the energy of disappointment, the energy of fear. When it's not solidified in one direction or another, that very energy pierces us to the heart, and it opens us. This is the discovery of egolessness. It's when all our usual schemes fall apart. Reaching our limit is like finding a doorway to sanity and the unconditional goodness of humanity, rather than meeting

23

an obstacle or a punishment.

The safest and most nurturing place to begin working this way is during formal meditation. On the cushion, we begin to get the hang of not indulging or repressing and of what it feels like to let the energy just be there. That is why it's so good to meditate every single day and continue to make friends with our hopes and fears again and again. This sows the seeds that enable us to be more awake in the midst of everyday chaos. It's a gradual awakening, and it's cumulative, but that's actually what happens. We don't sit in meditation to become good meditators. We sit in meditation so that we'll be more awake in our lives.

The first thing that happens in meditation is that we start to see what's happening. Even though we still run away and we still indulge, we see what we're doing clearly. One would think that our seeing it clearly would immediately make it just disappear, but it doesn't. So for quite a long time, we just see it clearly. To the degree that we're willing to see our indulging and our repressing clearly, they begin to wear themselves out. Wearing out is not exactly the same as going away. Instead, a wider, more generous, more enlightened perspective arises.

How we stay in the middle between indulging and repressing is by acknowledging whatever arises without judgment, letting the thoughts simply dissolve, and then going back to the openness of this very moment. That's what we're actually doing in meditation. Up come all these thoughts, but rather than squelch them or obsess with them, we acknowledge them and let them go. Then we come back to just being here. As Sogyal Rinpoche puts it, we simply "bring our mind back home."

After a while, that's how we relate with hope and fear in our daily lives. Out of nowhere, we stop struggling and relax. We stop talking to ourselves and come back to the freshness of the present moment.

This is something that evolves gradually, patiently, over time. How long does this process take? I would say it takes the rest of our lives. Basically, we're continually opening further, learning more, connecting further with the depths of human suffering and human wisdom, coming to know both those elements thoroughly and completely, and becoming more loving and compassionate people. And the teachings continue. There's always more to learn. We're not just complacent old fogies who've given up and aren't challenged by anything anymore. At the most surprising times, we still meet those ferocious dogs. We might think, as we become more open, that it's going to take bigger catastrophes for us to reach our limit. The interesting thing is that, as we open more and more, it's the big ones that immediately wake us up and the little things that catch us off guard. However, no matter what the size, color, or shape is, the point is still to lean toward the discomfort of life and see it clearly rather than to protect ourselves from it.

In practicing meditation, we're not trying to live up to some kind of ideal—quite the opposite. We're just being with our experience, whatever it is. If our experience is that sometimes we have some kind of perspective, and sometimes we have none, then that's our experience. If sometimes we can approach what scares us, and sometimes we absolutely can't, then that's our experience. "This very moment is the perfect teacher, and it's always with us" is really a most profound instruction. Just seeing what's going on—that's the teaching right there. We can be with what's happening and not dissociate. Awakeness is found in our pleasure and our pain, our confusion and our wisdom, available in each moment of our weird, unfathomable, ordinary everyday lives.

four

relax as it is

Once we know this instruction, we can put it into practice.
Then it's up to us what happens next. Ultimately, it comes down
to the question of just how willing we are to lighten up and
loosen our grip. How honest do we want to be with ourselves?

The meditation instruction that Chögyam Trungpa Rinpoche gave to his students is called *shamatha-vipashyana* meditation. When Trungpa Rinpoche first taught in the West, he told his students to simply open their minds and relax. If thoughts distracted them, they could simply let the thoughts dissolve and just come back to that open, relaxed state of mind.

After a few years, Rinpoche realized that some of the people who came to him found this simple instruction somewhat impossible to do and that they needed a bit more technique in order to proceed. At that point, without really changing the basic intent of the meditation, he nevertheless began to give the instructions a bit differently. He put more emphasis on posture and taught people to put very light attention on their out-breath. Later he said that the out-breath was as close as you could come to simply resting the mind in its natural open state and still have an object to which to return.

He emphasized that it should be just the ordinary out-breath, not manipulated in any way, and that the attention should be soft, a sort of touch-and-go approach. He said that about 25 percent of the attention should be on the breath, so that one was still aware of one's surroundings and didn't consider them an intrusion or an obstacle to meditation. Years later he used a humorous analogy comparing a meditator to someone all dressed up in a costume and holding a spoonful of water. One could be happily sitting there in one's fancy costume and still be quite undistracted from the spoonful of water in one's hand. The point was not to try to achieve some special state or to transcend the sounds and movement of ordinary life. Rather we were encouraged to relax more completely with our environment and to appreciate the world around us and the ordinary truth that takes place in every moment.

Most meditation techniques use an object of meditation—something you return to again and again no matter what's going on in your mind. Through rain, hail, snow, and sleet, fair weather and foul, you simply return to the object of meditation. In this case, the out-breath is the object of meditation—the elusive, fluid, everchanging out-breath, ungraspable and yet continuously arising. When you breathe in, it's like a pause or a gap. There is nothing particular to do except wait for the next out-breath.

I once explained this technique to a friend who had spent years doing a very focused concentration on both the in- and out-breaths as well as another object. When she heard this instruction, she said, "But that's impossible! No one could do this! There's a whole part where there's nothing to be aware of!" That was the first time I realized that built right into the instruction was the opportunity to completely let go. I'd heard Zen teachers talk of meditation as the willingness to die over and over again. And there it was—as each breath went out and dissolved, there was the chance to die to all that had gone before and to relax instead of panic.

Rinpoche asked us as meditation instructors not to speak of "concentrating" on the out-breath but to use more fluid language. So we would tell students to "touch the out-breath and let it go" or to "have a light and gentle attention on the out-breath" or "to be one with the breath as it relaxes outward." The basic guideline was still to open and relax without adding anything extra, without conceptualizing, but to keep returning to the mind just as it is, clear, lucid, and fresh.

After some time, Rinpoche added another refinement to the instruction. He began to ask us to label our thoughts "thinking." We'd be sitting there with the out-breath, and before we knew what had happened, we were gone—planning, worrying, fantasizing—completely in another world, a world totally made of thoughts. At the point when we realized we'd gone off, we were instructed to say to ourselves "thinking" and, without making it a big deal, to simply return again to the out-breath.

I once saw someone do a dance about this. The dancer came on stage and sat in the meditation posture. In a few seconds, thoughts of passion began to arise. The dancer moved through the process, becoming more and more frenzied as just a tiny glimpse of passion began to escalate until it was a full-blown sexual fantasy. Then a small bell rang, and a calm voice said "thinking," and the dancer relaxed back into the meditation posture. About five seconds later, the dance of rage began, again starting as a small irritation and then exploding more and more wildly. Then came the dance of loneliness, then the dance of drowsiness, and each time the bell would ring, and the voice would say "thinking," and the dancer would simply relax for a little longer and a little longer into what began to feel like the immense peace and spaciousness of simply sitting there.

Saying "thinking" is a very interesting point in the meditation. It's the point at which we can consciously train in gentleness and in developing a nonjudgmental attitude. The word for loving-kindness in Sanskrit is *maitri*. Maitri is also translated as unconditional friendliness. So each time you say to yourself "thinking," you are cultivating that unconditional friendliness toward whatever arises in your mind. Since this kind of unconditional compassion is difficult to come by, this simple and direct method for awakening it is exceedingly precious.

Sometimes we feel guilty, sometimes arrogant. Sometimes our thoughts and memories terrify us and make us feel totally miserable. Thoughts go through our minds all the time, and when we sit, we are providing a lot of space for all of them to arise. Like clouds in a big sky or waves in a vast sea, all our thoughts are given the space to appear. If one hangs on and sweeps us away, whether we call it pleasant or unpleasant, the instruction is to label it all "thinking" with as much openness and kindness as we can muster and let it dissolve back into the big sky. When the clouds and waves immediately return, it's no problem. We just acknowledge them again and again with unconditional friendliness, labeling them as just "thinking" and letting them go again and again and again.

Sometimes people use meditation to try to avoid bad feelings and disturbing thoughts. We might try to use the labeling as a way to get rid of what bothers us, and if we connect with something blissful or inspiring, we might think we've finally *got* it and try to stay where there's peace and harmony and nothing to fear.

So right from the beginning it's helpful to always remind yourself that meditation is about opening and relaxing with whatever arises, without picking and choosing. It's definitely not meant to repress anything, and it's not intended to encourage grasping, either. Allen Ginsberg uses the expression "surprise mind." You sit down and—wham!—a rather nasty surprise arises. Okay. So be it. This part is not to be rejected but compassionately acknowledged as "thinking" and let go. Then—wow!—a very delicious surprise appears. Okay. So be it. This part is not to be clung to but compassionately acknowledged as "thinking" and let go. These surprises are, we find, endless. Milarepa, the twelfth-century Tibetan yogi, sang wonderful songs about the proper way to meditate. In one song he says that mind has more projections than there are dust motes in a sunbeam and that even hundreds of spears couldn't put an end to that. So as meditators we might as well stop struggling against our thoughts and realize that honesty and humor are far more inspiring and helpful than any kind of solemn religious striving for or against anything.

In any case, the point is not to try to get rid of thoughts, but rather to see their true nature. Thoughts will run us around in circles if we buy into them, but really they are like dream images. They are like an illusion—not really all that solid. They are, as we say, just thinking.

Over the years, Rinpoche continued to refine the instructions on posture. He said it was never a good idea to struggle in meditation. So if our legs or back were hurting, we were told it was fine to move. However, it became clear that by working with proper posture, it was possible to become far more relaxed and settled in one's body by making very subtle adjustments. Large movements brought comfort for about five or ten minutes, and then we just wanted to shift again. Eventually we began following the six points of good posture as a way to really settle down. The six points are:

1. seat, 2. legs, 3. torso, 4. hands, 5. eyes, and 6. mouth, and the instruction is as follows.

1. Whether sitting on a cushion on the floor or in a chair, the seat should be flat, not tilting to the right or left or to the back or front.
2. The legs are crossed comfortably in front of you—or, if you're sitting in a chair, the feet are flat on the floor, and the knees are a few inches apart.
3. The torso (from the head to the seat) is upright, with a strong back and an open front. If sitting in a chair, it's best not to lean back. If you start to slouch, simply sit upright again.
4. The hands are open, with palms down, resting on the thighs.
5. The eyes are open, indicating the attitude of remaining awake and relaxed with all that occurs. The eye gaze is slightly downward and directed about four to six feet in front.
6. The mouth is very slightly open so that the jaw is relaxed and air can move easily through both mouth and nose. The tip of the tongue can be placed on the roof of the mouth.

Each time you sit down to meditate, you can run through these six points, and anytime you feel distracted during your meditation, you can bring your attention back to your body and run through the six points. Then, with a sense of starting afresh, return once again to the out-breath. If you find that thoughts have carried you away, don't worry about it. Simply say to yourself, "thinking," and come back to the openness and relaxation of the out-breath. Again and again just come back to being right where you are.

In the beginning people sometimes find this meditation exciting. It's like a new project, and you think that if you do it, perhaps all the unwanted stuff will go away and you'll become open, nonjudgmental, and unconditionally friendly. But after a while the sense of project wears out. You just find time each day, and you sit down with yourself. You come back to that breath over and over, through boredom, edginess, fear, and well-being. This perseverance and repetition—when done with honesty, a light touch, humor, and kindness—is its own reward.

Once we know this instruction, we can put it into practice. Then it's up to us what happens next. Ultimately, it comes down to the question of just how willing we are to lighten up and loosen our grip. How honest do we want to be with ourselves?

five

it's never too late

What makes maitri such a different approach is that we are not
trying to solve a problem. We are not striving to make pain go
away or to become a better person. In fact, we are giving up
control altogether and letting concepts and ideals fall apart.

I get many letters from "the worst person in the world." Sometimes this worst person is getting older and feels he has wasted his life. Sometimes she is a suicidal teenager reaching out for help. The people who give themselves such a hard time come in all ages, shapes, and colors. The thing they have in common is that they have no loving-kindness for themselves.

Recently I was talking with a man I've known for a long time. I've always considered him to be a shy, good-hearted person who spends more time than most helping other people. On this day he was completely despondent and feeling like a hopeless case. Intending to be facetious, I asked him, "Well, don't you think that somewhere on this planet there might be someone worse than you?" He answered with heartbreaking honesty, "No. If you want to know what I really feel, it's that there's no one as bad as me."

It made me think of a Gary Larson cartoon I once saw. Two women are standing behind their locked door peeking out the window at a monster standing on their doorstep. One of the ladies is saying, "Calm down, Edna. Yes, it is a giant hideous insect, but it may be a giant hideous insect in need of help."

The most difficult times for many of us are the ones we give ourselves. Yet it's never too late or too early to practice loving-kindness. It's as if we had a terminal disease but might live for quite a while. Not knowing how much time we have left, we might begin to think it was important to make friends with ourselves and others in the remaining hours, months, or years.

It is said that we can't attain enlightenment, let alone feel contentment and joy, without seeing who we are and what we do, without seeing our patterns and our habits. This is called maitri—developing loving-kindness and an unconditional friendship with ourselves.

People sometimes confuse this process with self-improvement or building themselves up. We can get so caught up in being good to ourselves that we don't pay any attention at all to the impact that we're having on others. We might erroneously believe that maitri is a way to find a happiness that lasts; as advertisements so seductively promise, we could feel great for the rest of our lives. It's not that we pat ourselves on the back and say, "You're the greatest," or "Don't worry, sweetheart, everything is going to be fine." Rather it's a process by which self-deception becomes so skillfully and compassionately exposed that there's no mask that can hide us anymore.

What makes maitri such a different approach is that we are not trying to solve a problem. We are not striving to make pain go away or to become a better person. In fact, we are giving up control altogether and letting concepts and ideals fall apart.

This starts with realizing that whatever occurs is neither the beginning nor the end. It is just the same kind of normal human experience that's been happening to everyday people from the beginning of time. Thoughts, emotions, moods, and memories come and they go, and basic nowness is always here.

It is never too late for any of us to look at our minds. We can always sit down and allow the space for anything to arise. Sometimes we have a shocking experience of ourselves. Sometimes we try to hide. Sometimes we have a surprising experience of ourselves. Often we get carried away. Without judging, without buying into likes and dislikes, we can always encourage ourselves to just be here again and again and again.

The painful thing is that when we buy into disapproval, we are practicing disapproval. When we buy into harshness, we are practicing harshness. The more we do it, the stronger these qualities become. How sad it is that we become so expert at causing harm to ourselves and others. The trick then is to practice gentleness and letting go. We can learn to meet whatever arises with curiosity and not make it such a big deal. Instead of struggling against the force of confusion, we could meet it and relax.

When we do that, we gradually discover that clarity is always there. In the middle of the worst scenario of the worst person in the world, in the midst of all the heavy dialogue with ourselves, open space is always there.

We carry around an image of ourselves, an image we hold in our minds. One way to describe this is "small mind." It can also be described as *sem*. In Tibetan there are several words for mind, but two that are particularly helpful to know are *sem* and *rikpa*. Sem is what we experience as discursive thoughts, a stream of chatter that's always reinforcing an image of ourselves. Rikpa literally means "intelligence" or "brightness." Behind all the planning and worrying, behind all the wishing and wanting, picking and choosing, the unfabricated, wisdom mind of rikpa is always here. Whenever we stop talking to ourselves, rikpa is continually here.

In Nepal the dogs bark all night long. Every twenty minutes or so, they all stop at once, and there is an experience of immense relief and stillness. Then they all start barking again. The small mind of sem can feel just like that. When we first start meditating, it's as if the dogs never stop barking at all. After a while, there are those gaps. Discursive thoughts are rather like wild dogs that need taming. Rather than beating them or throwing stones, we tame them with compassion. Over and over we regard them with the precision and kindness that allow them to gradually calm down. Sometimes it feels like there's much more space, with just a few yips and yaps here and there.

Of course the noise will continue. We aren't trying to get rid of those dogs. But once we've touched in with the spaciousness of rikpa, it begins to permeate everything. Once we've even had a glimpse of spaciousness, if we practice with maitri, it will continue to expand. It expands into our resentment. It expands into our fear. It expands into our concepts and opinions about things and into who we think we are. We might sometimes even get the feeling that life is like a dream.

When I was about ten, my best friend started having nightmares: she'd be running through a huge dark building pursued by hideous monsters. She'd get to a door, struggle to open it, and no sooner had she closed it behind her than she'd hear it opened by the rapidly approaching monsters. Finally she'd wake up screaming and crying for help.

One day we were sitting in her kitchen talking about her nightmares. When I asked her what the demons looked like, she said she didn't know because she was always running away. After I asked her that question, she began to wonder about the monsters. She wondered if any of them looked like witches and if any of them had knives. So on the next occurrence of the nightmare, just as the demons began to pursue her, she stopped running and turned around. It took tremendous courage, and her heart was pounding, but she put her back up against the wall and looked at them. They all stopped right in front of her and began jumping up and down, but none of them came closer. There were five in all, each looking something like an animal. One of them was a gray bear, but instead of claws, it had long red fingernails. One had four eyes. Another had a wound on its cheek. Once she looked closely, they appeared less like monsters and more like the two-dimensional drawings in comic books. Then slowly they began to fade. After that she woke up, and that was the end of her nightmares.

There is a teaching on the three kinds of awakening: awakening from the dream of ordinary sleep, awakening at death from the dream of life, and awakening into full enlightenment from the dream of delusion. These teachings say that when we die, we experience it as waking up from a very long dream. When I heard this teaching, I remembered my friend's nightmares. It struck me right then that if all this is really a dream, I might as well spend it trying to look at what scares me instead of running away. I haven't always found this all that easy to do, but in the process I've learned a lot about maitri.

Our personal demons come in many guises. We experience them as shame, as jealousy, as abandonment, as rage. They are anything that makes us so uncomfortable that we continually run away.

We do the big escape: we act out, say something, slam a door, hit someone, or throw a pot as a way of not facing what's happening in our hearts. Or we shove the feelings under and somehow deaden the pain. We can spend our whole lives escaping from the monsters of our minds.

All over the world, people are so caught in running that they forget to take advantage of the beauty around them. We become so accustomed to speeding ahead that we rob ourselves of joy.

Once I dreamt that I was getting a house ready for Khandro Rinpoche. I was rushing around cleaning and cooking. Suddenly her car drove up, and there she was with her attendant. As I ran up and greeted them, Rinpoche smiled at me and asked, "Did you see the sun come up this morning?" I answered, "No, Rinpoche, I didn't. I was much too busy to see the sun." She laughed and said, "Too busy to live life!"

Sometimes it seems we have a preference for darkness and speed. We can protest and complain and hold a grudge for a thousand years. But in the midst of the bitterness and resentment, we have a glimpse of the possibility of maitri. We hear a child crying or smell that someone is baking bread. We feel the coolness of the air or see the first crocus of spring. Despite ourselves we are drawn out by the beauty in our own backyard.

The way to dissolve our resistance to life is to meet it face to face. When we feel resentment because the room is too hot, we could meet the heat and feel its fieriness and its heaviness. When we feel resentment because the room is too cold, we could meet the cold and feel its iciness and its bite. When we want to complain about the rain, we could feel its wetness instead. When we worry because the wind is shaking our windows, we could meet the wind and hear its sound. Cutting our expectations for a cure is a gift we can give ourselves. There is no cure for hot and cold. They will go on forever. After we have died, the ebb and flow will still continue. Like the tides of the sea, like day and night—this is the nature of things. Being able to appreciate, being able to look closely, being able to open our minds—this is the core of maitri.

When the rivers and air are polluted, when families and nations are at war, when homeless wanderers fill the highways, these are traditional signs of a dark age. Another is that people become poisoned by self-doubt and become cowards.

Practicing loving-kindness toward ourselves seems as good a way as any to start illuminating the darkness of difficult times.

Being preoccupied with our self-image is like being deaf and blind. It's like standing in the middle of a vast field of wildflowers with a black hood over our heads. It's like coming upon a tree of singing birds while wearing earplugs.

There's so much resentment and so much resistance to life. In all nations, it's like a plague that's gotten out of control and is poisoning the atmosphere of the world. At this point it might be wise to wonder about these things and begin to get the knack of loving-kindness.

six

not causing harm

It's a transformative experience to simply pause instead of
immediately filling up the space. By waiting, we begin to
connect with fundamental restlessness as well as
fundamental spaciousness.

Not causing harm obviously includes not killing
or robbing or lying to people. It also includes
not being aggressive—not being aggressive with
our actions, our speech, or our minds. Learning not to
cause harm to ourselves or others is a basic Buddhist
teaching on the healing power of nonaggression.

Not harming ourselves or others in the beginning, not
harming ourselves or others in the middle, and not harming ourselves or others in the end is the basis of enlightened society. This is how there could be a sane world. It
starts with sane citizens, and that is us. The most fundamental aggression to ourselves, the most fundamental
harm we can do to ourselves, is to remain ignorant by not
having the courage and the respect to look at ourselves
honestly and gently.

The ground of not causing harm is mindfulness, a

43

sense of clear seeing with respect and compassion for what it is we see. This is what basic practice shows us. But mindfulness doesn't stop with formal meditation. It helps us relate with all the details of our lives. It helps us see and hear and smell, without closing our eyes or our ears or our noses. It's a life-time's journey to relate honestly to the immediacy of our experience and to respect ourselves enough not to judge it.

As we become more wholehearted in this journey of gentle honesty, it comes as quite a shock to realize how much we've blinded ourselves to some of the ways in which we cause harm. Our style is so ingrained that we can't hear when people try to tell us, either kindly or rudely, that maybe we're causing some harm by the way we are or the way we relate with others. We've become so used to the way we do things that somehow we think that others are used to it too.

It's painful to face how we harm others, and it takes a while. It's a journey that happens because of our commitment to gentleness and honesty, our commitment to staying awake, to being mindful. Because of mindfulness, we see our desires and our aggression, our jealousy and our ignorance. We don't act on them; we just see them. Without mindfulness, we don't see them.

The next step is refraining. Mindfulness is the ground; refraining is the path. Refraining is one of those uptight words that sound repressive. Surely alive, juicy, interesting people would not practice refraining. Maybe they would sometimes refrain, but not as a lifestyle. In this context, however, refraining is very much the method of becoming a dharmic person. It's the quality of not grabbing for entertainment the minute we feel a slight edge of boredom coming on. It's the practice of not immediately filling up space just because there's a gap.

Once I was given an interesting meditation practice that combined mindfulness and refraining. We were told just to notice what our physical movements were when we felt uncomfortable. I began to notice that when I felt uncomfortable, I did things like pull my ear, scratch my nose or head when it didn't itch, or straighten my collar. I made all kinds of little jumpy, jittery movements when I felt like I was losing ground. Our instruction was not to try to change anything, not to criticize ourselves for whatever we were doing, but just to see what we did.

Noticing how we try to avoid it is a way to get in touch with basic groundlessness. Refraining—not habitually acting out impulsively—has something to do with giving up entertainment mentality. Through refraining, we see that there's something between the arising of the craving—or the aggression or the loneliness or whatever it might be—and whatever action we take as a result. There's something there in us that we don't want to experience, and we never do experience, because we're so quick to act.

Underneath our ordinary lives, underneath all the talking we do, all the moving we do, all the thoughts in our minds, there's a fundamental groundlessness. It's there bubbling along all the time. We experience it as restlessness and edginess. We experience it as fear. It motivates passion, aggression, ignorance, jealousy, and pride, but we never get down to the essence of it.

Refraining is the method for getting to know the nature of this restlessness and fear. It's a method for settling into groundlessness. If we immediately entertain ourselves by talking, by acting, by thinking—if there's never any pause—we will never be able to relax. We will always be speeding through our lives. We'll always be stuck with what my grandfather called a good case of the jitters. Refraining is a way of making friends with ourselves at the most profound level possible. We can begin to relate with what's underneath all the bubbles and burps and farts, all the stuff that comes out and expresses itself as uptight, controlling, manipulative behavior, or whatever it is. Underneath all that, there's something very soft, very tender, that we experience as fear or edginess.

Once there was a young warrior. Her teacher told her that she had to do battle with fear. She didn't want to do that. It seemed too aggressive; it was scary; it seemed unfriendly. But the teacher said she had to do it and gave her the instructions for the battle. The day arrived. The student warrior stood on one side, and fear stood on the other. The warrior was feeling very small, and fear was looking big and wrathful. They both had their weapons. The young warrior roused herself and went toward fear, prostrated three times, and asked, "May I have permission to go into battle with you?" Fear said, "Thank you for showing me so much respect that you ask permission." Then the young warrior said, "How can I defeat you?" Fear replied, "My weapons are that I talk fast, and I get very close to your face. Then you get completely unnerved, and you do whatever I say. If you don't do what I tell you, I have no power. You can listen to me, and you can have respect for me. You can even be convinced by me. But if you don't do what I say, I have no power." In that way, the student warrior learned how to defeat fear.

This is how it actually works. There has to be some kind of respect for the jitters, some understanding of how our emotions have the power to run us around in circles. That understanding helps us discover how we increase our pain, how we increase our confusion, how we cause harm to ourselves. Because we have basic goodness, basic wisdom, basic intelligence, we can stop harming ourselves and harming others. Because of mindfulness, we see things when they arise. Because of our understanding, we don't buy into the chain reaction that makes things grow from minute to expansive. We leave things minute. They stay tiny. They don't keep expanding into World War III or domestic violence. It all comes through learning to pause for a moment, learning not to just impulsively do the same thing again and again. It's a transformative experience to simply pause instead of immediately filling up the space. By waiting, we begin to connect with fundamental restlessness as well as fundamental spaciousness.

The result is that we cease to cause harm. We begin to know ourselves thoroughly and to respect ourselves. Anything can come up, anything can walk into our house; we can find anything sitting on our living-room couch, and we don't freak out. We have been thoroughly processed by coming to know ourselves, thoroughly processed by this honest, gentle mindfulness.

This process connects us with the fruition of not causing harm—fundamental well-being of our body, speech, and mind. Well-being of body is like a mountain. A lot happens on a mountain. It hails, and the winds come up, and it rains and snows. The sun gets very hot, clouds cross over, animals shit and piss on the mountain, and so do people. People leave their trash, and other people clean it up. Many things come and go on this mountain, but it just sits there. When we've seen ourselves completely, there's a stillness of body that is like a mountain. We no longer get jumpy and have to scratch our noses, pull our ears, punch somebody, go running from the room, or drink ourselves into oblivion. A thoroughly good relationship with ourselves results in being still, which doesn't mean we don't run and jump and dance about. It means there's no compulsiveness. We don't overwork, overeat, oversmoke, overseduce. In short, we begin to stop causing harm.

Well-being of speech is like a lute without strings. Even without strings, the musical instrument proclaims itself. This is an image of our speech being settled. It doesn't mean that we're controlling, uptight, trying hard not to say the wrong thing. It means that our speech is straightforward and disciplined. We don't start blurting out words just because no one else is talking and we're nervous. We don't chatter away like magpies and crows.

We've heard it all; we've been insulted and we've been praised. We know what it is to be in situations where everyone is angry, where everyone is peaceful. We're at home in the world because we're at home with ourselves, so we don't feel that out of nervousness, out of our habitual pattern, we have to run at the mouth. Our speech is tamed, and when we speak, it communicates. We don't waste the gift of speech in expressing our neurosis.

Well-being of mind is like a mountain lake without ripples. When the lake has no ripples, everything in the lake can be seen. When the water is all churned up, nothing can be seen. The still lake without ripples is an image of our minds at ease, so full of unlimited friendliness for all the junk at the bottom of the lake that we don't feel the need to churn up the waters just to avoid looking at what's there.

Not causing harm requires staying awake. Part of being awake is slowing down enough to notice what we say and do. The more we witness our emotional chain reactions and understand how they work, the easier it is to refrain. It becomes a way of life to stay awake, slow down, and notice.

At the root of all the harm we cause is ignorance. Through meditation, that's what we begin to undo. If we see that we have no mindfulness, that we rarely refrain, that we have little well-being, that is not confusion, that's the beginning of clarity. As the moments of our lives go by, our ability to be deaf, dumb, and blind just doesn't work so well anymore. Rather than making us more uptight, interestingly enough, this process liberates us. This is the liberation that naturally arises when we are completely here, without anxiety about imperfection.

seven

hopelessness
and death

*If we're willing to give up hope that insecurity and pain
can be exterminated, then we can have the courage to
relax with the groundlessness of our situation.
This is the first step on the path.*

Turning your mind toward the dharma does not
bring security or confirmation. Turning your mind
toward the dharma does not bring any ground
to stand on. In fact, when your mind turns toward the
dharma, you fearlessly acknowledge impermanence and
change and begin to get the knack of hopelessness.

In Tibetan there's an interesting word: *ye tang che*. The
ye part means "totally, completely," and the rest of it
means "exhausted." Altogether, *ye tang che* means totally
tired out. We might say "totally fed up." It describes an
experience of complete hopelessness, of completely giving
up hope. This is an important point. This is the beginning
of the beginning. Without giving up hope—that there's
somewhere better to be, that there's someone better to

be—we will never relax with where we are or who we are.

We could say that the word *mindfulness* is pointing to being one with our experience, not dissociating, being right there when our hand touches the doorknob or the telephone rings or feelings of all kinds arise. The word *mindfulness* describes being right where we are. *Ye tang che*, however, is not so easily digested. It expresses the renunciation that's essential for the spiritual path.

To think that we can finally get it all together is unrealistic. To seek for some lasting security is futile. To undo our very ancient and very stuck habitual patterns of mind requires that we begin to turn around some of our most basic assumptions. Believing in a solid, separate self, continuing to seek pleasure and avoid pain, thinking that someone "out there" is to blame for our pain—one has to get totally fed up with these ways of thinking. One has to give up hope that this way of thinking will bring us satisfaction. Suffering begins to dissolve when we can question the belief or the hope that there's anywhere to hide.

Hopelessness means that we no longer have the spirit for holding our trip together. We may still *want* to hold our trip together. We long to have some reliable, comfortable ground under our feet, but we've tried a thousand ways to hide and a thousand ways to tie up all the loose ends, and the ground just keeps moving under us. Trying to get lasting security teaches us a lot, because if we never try to do it, we never notice that it can't be done. Turning our minds toward the dharma speeds up the process of discovery. At

every turn we realize once again that it's completely hopeless—we can't get any ground under our feet.

The difference between theism and nontheism is not
whether one does or does not believe in God. It is an
issue that applies to everyone, including both Buddhists
and non-Buddhists. Theism is a deep-seated conviction
that there's some hand to hold: if we just do the right
things, someone will appreciate us and take care of us.
It means thinking there's always going to be a babysitter
available when we need one. We all are inclined to abdi-
cate our responsibilities and delegate our authority to
something outside ourselves. Nontheism is relaxing with
the ambiguity and uncertainty of the present moment
without reaching for anything to protect ourselves. We
sometimes think that dharma is something outside of
ourselves—something to believe in, something to measure up to. However, dharma isn't a belief; it isn't dogma. It
is total appreciation of impermanence and change. The
teachings disintegrate when we try to grasp them. We
have to experience them without hope. Many brave and
compassionate people have experienced them and taught
them. The message is fearless; dharma was never meant
to be a belief that we blindly follow. Dharma gives us
nothing to hold on to at all.

Nontheism is finally realizing that there's no babysitter
that you can count on. You just get a good one and then
he or she is gone. Nontheism is realizing that it's not just
babysitters that come and go. The whole of life is like that.
This is the truth, and the truth is inconvenient.

For those who want something to hold on to, life is even more inconvenient. From this point of view, theism is an addiction. We're all addicted to hope—hope that the doubt and mystery will go away. This addiction has a painful effect on society: a society based on lots of people addicted to getting ground under their feet is not a very compassionate place.

The first noble truth of the Buddha is that when we feel suffering, it doesn't mean that something is wrong. What a relief. Finally somebody told the truth. Suffering is part of life, and we don't have to feel it's happening because we personally made the wrong move. In reality, however, when we feel suffering, we think that something *is* wrong. As long as we're addicted to hope, we feel that we can tone our experience down or liven it up or change it somehow, and we continue to suffer a lot.

The word in Tibetan for hope is *rewa*; the word for fear is *dokpa*. More commonly, the word *re-dok* is used, which combines the two. Hope and fear is a feeling with two sides. As long as there's one, there's always the other. This *re-dok* is the root of our pain. In the world of hope and fear, we always have to change the channel, change the temperature, change the music, because something is getting uneasy, something is getting restless, something is beginning to hurt, and we keep looking for alternatives.

In a nontheistic state of mind, abandoning hope is an affirmation, the beginning of the beginning. You could even put "Abandon hope" on your refrigerator door instead of more conventional aspirations like "Every day in every way I'm getting better and better."

Hope and fear come from feeling that we lack something; they come from a sense of poverty. We can't simply relax with ourselves. We hold on to hope, and hope robs us of the present moment. We feel that someone else knows what's going on, but that there's something missing in us, and therefore something is lacking in our world.

Rather than letting our negativity get the better of us, we could acknowledge that right now we feel like a piece of shit and not be squeamish about taking a good look. That's the compassionate thing to do. That's the brave thing to do. We could smell that piece of shit. We could feel it; what is its texture, color, and shape?

We can explore the nature of that piece of shit. We can know the nature of dislike, shame, and embarrassment and not believe there's something wrong with that. We can drop the fundamental hope that there is a better "me" who one day will emerge. We can't just jump over ourselves as if we were not there. It's better to take a straight look at all our hopes and fears. Then some kind of confidence in our basic sanity arises.

This is where renunciation enters the picture—renunciation of the hope that our experience could be different, renunciation of the hope that we could be better. The Buddhist monastic rules that advise renouncing liquor, renouncing sex, and so on are not pointing out that those things are inherently bad or immoral, but that we use them as babysitters. We use them as a way to escape; we use them to try to get comfort and to distract ourselves.

The real thing that we renounce is the tenacious hope that we could be saved from being who we are. Renunciation is a teaching to inspire us to investigate what's happening every time we grab something because we can't stand to face what's coming.

Once I was sitting next to a man on an airplane who kept interrupting our conversation to take various pills. I asked him, "What is that you're taking?" He answered that they were tranquilizers. I said, "Oh, are you nervous?" and he said, "No, not now, but I think when I get home I'm going to be."

You can laugh at this story, but what happens with *you* when you begin to feel uneasy, unsettled, queasy? Notice the panic, notice when you instantly grab for something. That grabbing is based on hope. Not grabbing is called hopelessness.

If hope and fear are two sides of one coin, so are hopelessness and confidence. If we're willing to give up hope that insecurity and pain can be exterminated, then we can have the courage to relax with the groundlessness of our situation. This is the first step on the path. If there is no interest in stepping beyond hope and fear, then there's no meaning in taking refuge in the buddha, the dharma, and the sangha. Taking refuge in the buddha, dharma, and sangha is about giving up hope of getting ground under our feet. We are ready to take refuge when this style of teaching—whether we feel completely up to it or not—is like hearing something hauntingly familiar, like the experience of a child meeting its mother after a long separation.

Hopelessness is the basic ground. Otherwise, we're going to make the journey with the hope of getting security. If we make the journey to get security, we're completely missing the point. We can do our meditation practice with the hope of getting security; we can study the teachings with the hope of getting security; we can follow all the guidelines and instructions with the hope of getting security; but it will only lead to disappointment and pain. We could save ourselves a lot of time by taking this message very seriously right now. Begin the journey without hope of getting ground under your feet. Begin with hopelessness.

All anxiety, all dissatisfaction, all the reasons for hoping that our experience could be different are rooted in our fear of death. Fear of death is always in the background. As the Zen master Shunryu Suzuki Roshi said, life is like getting into a boat that's just about to sail out to sea and sink. But it's very hard—no matter how much we hear about it—to believe in our own death. Many spiritual practices try to encourage us to take our own death seriously, but it's amazing how difficult it is to allow it to hit home. The one thing in life that we can really count on is incredibly remote for all of us. We don't go so far as to say, "No way, I'm not going to die," because of course we know that we are. But it definitely will be later. That's the biggest hope.

Trungpa Rinpoche once gave a public lecture titled "Death in Everyday Life." We are raised in a culture that fears death and hides it from us. Nevertheless, we experience it all the time. We experience it in the form of disappointment, in the form of things not working out. We experience it in the form of things always being in a process of change. When the day ends, when the second ends, when we breathe out, that's death in everyday life.

Death in everyday life could also be defined as experiencing all the things that we don't want. Our marriage isn't working; our job isn't coming together. Having a relationship with death in everyday life means that we begin to be able to wait, to relax with insecurity, with panic, with embarrassment, with things not working out. As the years go on, we don't call the babysitter quite so fast.

Death and hopelessness provide proper motivation— proper motiviation for living an insightful, compassionate life. But most of the time, warding off death is our biggest motivation. We habitually ward off any sense of problem. We're always trying to deny that it's a natural occurrence that things change, that the sand is slipping through our fingers. Time is passing. It's as natural as the seasons changing and day turning into night. But getting old, getting sick, losing what we love—we don't see those events as natural occurrences. We want to ward off that sense of death, no matter what.

When we have reminders of death, we panic. It isn't just that we cut our finger, blood begins to flow, and we put on a Band-Aid. We add something extra—our style. Some of us just sit there stoically and bleed all over our clothes. Some of us get hysterical; we don't just get a Band-Aid, we call the ambulance and go to the hospital.

Some of us put on designer Band-Aids. But whatever our style is, it's not simple. It's not bare bones.

Can't we just return to the bare bones? Can't we just come back? That's the beginning of the beginning. Bare bones, good old self. Bare bones, good old bloody finger. Come back to square one, just the minimum bare bones. Relaxing with the present moment, relaxing with hopelessness, relaxing with death, not resisting the fact that things end, that things pass, that things have no lasting substance, that everything is changing all the time—that is the basic message.

When we talk about hopelessness and death, we're talking about facing the facts. No escapism. We may still have addictions of all kinds, but we cease to believe in them as a gateway to happiness. So many times we've indulged the short-term pleasure of addiction. We've done it so many times that we know that grasping at this hope is a source of misery that makes a short-term pleasure a long-term hell.

Giving up hope is encouragement to stick with yourself, to make friends with yourself, to not run away from yourself, to return to the bare bones, no matter what's going on. Fear of death is the background of the whole thing. It's why we feel restless, why we panic, why there's anxiety. But if we totally experience hopelessness, giving up all hope of alternatives to the present moment, we can have a joyful relationship with our lives, an honest, direct relationship, one that no longer ignores the reality of impermanence and death.

eight

eight worldly dharmas

We might feel that somehow we should try to eradicate these
feelings of pleasure and pain, loss and gain, praise and blame,
fame and disgrace. A more practical approach would be to get
to know them, see how they hook us, see how they color our
perception of reality, see how they aren't all that solid. Then
the eight worldly dharmas become the means for growing
wiser as well as kinder and more content.

One of the classic Buddhist teachings on hope
and fear concerns what are known as the eight
worldly dharmas. These are four pairs of opposites—four things that we like and become attached to
and four things that we don't like and try to avoid. The
basic message is that when we are caught up in the eight
worldly dharmas, we suffer.

First, we like pleasure; we are attached to it. Con-
versely, we don't like pain. Second, we like and are
attached to praise. We try to avoid criticism and
blame. Third, we like and are attached to fame. We

dislike and try to avoid disgrace. Finally, we are attached to gain, to getting what we want. We don't like losing what we have.

According to this very simple teaching, becoming immersed in these four pairs of opposites—pleasure and pain, loss and gain, fame and disgrace, and praise and blame—is what keeps us stuck in the pain of samsara.

Whenever we're feeling good, our thoughts are usually about things we like—praise, gain, pleasure, and fame. When we're feeling uncomfortable and irritable and fed up, our thoughts and emotions are probably revolving around something like pain, loss, disgrace, or blame.

Let's take praise and blame. Someone walks up to us and says, "You are old." If it just so happens that we want to be old, we feel really good. We feel as if we've just been praised. That gives us enormous pleasure and a sense of gain and fame. But suppose we have been obsessing all year about getting rid of wrinkles and firming up our jaw line. When someone says, "You are old," we feel insulted. We've just been blamed, and we feel a corresponding sense of pain.

Even if we don't talk about this particular teaching any further, we can already see that many of our mood swings are related to how we interpret what happens. If we look closely at our mood swings, we'll notice that something always sets them off. We carry around a subjective reality that is continually triggering our emotional reactions. Someone says, "You are old," and we enter into a particular state of mind—either happy or sad, delighted or angry.

For someone else, the same experience might be completely neutral.

Words are spoken, letters are received, phone calls are made, food is eaten, things appear or don't appear. We wake up in the morning, we open our eyes, and events happen all day long, until we go to sleep. A lot is happening in our sleep, too. All night long we encounter the people and events of our dreams. How do we react to what occurs? Are we attached to certain kinds of experiences? Do we reject or avoid others? How hooked do we get by these eight worldly dharmas?

The irony is that we make up the eight worldly dharmas. We make them up in reaction to what happens to us in this world. They are nothing concrete in themselves. Even more strange is that we are not all that solid either. We have a concept of ourselves that we reconstruct moment by moment and reflexively try to protect. But this concept that we are protecting is questionable. It's all "much ado about nothing"—like pushing and pulling a vanishing illusion.

We might feel that somehow we should try to eradicate these feelings of pleasure and pain, loss and gain, praise and blame, fame and disgrace. A more practical approach would be to get to know them, see how they hook us, see how they color our perception of reality, see how they aren't all that solid. Then the eight worldly dharmas become the means for growing wiser as well as kinder and more content.

To begin with, in meditation we can notice how emotions

and moods are connected with having lost or gained something, having been praised or blamed, and so forth. We can notice how what begins as a simple thought, a simple quality of energy, quickly blossoms into full-blown pleasure and pain. We have to have a certain amount of fearlessness, of course, because we like it all to come out on the pleasure/praise/fame/gain side. We like to ensure that everything will come out in our favor. But when we really look, we're going to see that we have no control over what occurs at all. We have all kinds of mood swings and emotional reactions. They just come and go endlessly.

Sometimes we're going to find ourselves completely caught up in a drama. We're going to be just as angry as if someone had just walked into the room and slapped us in the face. Then it might occur to us: "Wait a minute— what's going on here?" We look into it and are able to see that, out of no-where, we feel that we have lost something or been insulted. Where this thought came from we don't know, but here we are, hooked again by the eight worldly dharmas.

Right then, we can feel that energy, do our best to let the thoughts dissolve, and give ourselves a break. Beyond all that fuss and bother is a big sky. Right there in the middle of the tempest, we can drop it and relax.

Or we might be completely caught up in a delightful, pleasurable fantasy. We look into it and see that, out of nowhere, we feel we have gained something, won some-thing, been praised for something. What pops up is out of our control, totally unpredictable, like the images in a dream. But up it comes, and we're hooked again by the eight worldly dharmas.

The human race is so predictable. A tiny thought arises, then escalates, and before we know what hit us, we're caught up in hope and fear.

In the eighth century a remarkable man introduced Buddhism into Tibet. His name was Padmasambhava, the Lotus-Born. He is also called Guru Rinpoche. The legend is that he simply appeared one morning sitting on a lotus in the middle of a lake. It is said that this unusual child was born completely awake, knowing from the very first moment that phenomena—both outer and inner—have no reality at all. What he didn't know was how everyday things functioned in his world.

He was a very inquisitive boy. He found out on the first day that because of his radiance and beauty, everyone was attracted to him. He saw too that when he was joyful and playful, people were happy and showered him with praise. The king of this country was so taken with the child that he took Guru Rinpoche to live in the palace and treated him like a son.

Then one day the boy went up to play on the flat roof of the palace, taking with him the king's ritual instruments, a bell and a metal scepter called a *vajra*. Completely delighted, he danced around on the rooftop, ringing the bell and spinning the vajra. Then with great curiosity, he tossed them into space. They fell to the street below, landing on the heads of two passersby and killing them instantly.

The people of the country were so outraged that they demanded that the king exile Guru Rinpoche. That very day, without any baggage or food, he was sent off into the wilderness alone.

This inquisitive child had learned a powerful lesson about the workings of the world. The story goes that this brief but vivid encounter with praise and blame was all he needed to figure out the everyday operations of samsara. From then on he abandoned hope and fear and worked joyfully to awaken others.

We can also use our lives this way. We can explore these familiar pairs of opposites in everything we do. Instead of automatically falling into habitual patterns, we can begin to notice how we react when someone praises us. When someone blames us, how do we react? When we've lost something, how do we react? When we feel we've gained something, how do we react? When we feel pleasure or pain, is it as simple as that? Do we just feel pleasure or pain? Or is there a whole libretto that goes along with it?

When we become inquisitive about these things, look into them, see who we are and what we do, with the curiosity of a young child, what might seem like a problem becomes a source of wisdom. Oddly enough, this curiosity begins to undercut what we call ego pain or self-centeredness, and we see more clearly. Usually we're just swept along by the pleasant or painful feelings. We're swept away by them in both directions; we spin off in our habitual style, and we don't even notice what's happening.

Before we know it, we've composed a novel on why some-one is so wrong, or why we are so right, or why we must get such-and-such. When we begin to understand the whole process, it begins to lighten up considerably.

We are like children building a sand castle. We embel-lish it with beautiful shells, bits of driftwood, and pieces of colored glass. The castle is ours, off-limits to others. We're willing to attack if others threaten to hurt it. Yet despite all our attachment, we know that the tide will inevitably come in and sweep the sand castle away. The trick is to enjoy it fully but without clinging, and when the time comes, let it dissolve back into the sea.

This letting things go is sometimes called non attach-ment, but not with the cool, remote quality often asso-ciated with that word. This nonattachment has more kindness and more intimacy than that. It's actually a desire to know, like the questions of a three-year-old. We want to know our pain so we can stop endlessly running. We want to know our pleasure so we can stop endlessly grasping. Then somehow our questions get bigger and our inquisitiveness more vast. We want to know about loss so we might understand other people when their lives are falling apart. We want to know about gain so we might understand other people when they are delighted or when they get arrogant and puffed up and carried away.

When we become more insightful and compassionate about how we ourselves get hooked, we spontaneously feel more tenderness for the human race. Knowing our own confusion, we're more willing and able to get our hands dirty and try to alleviate the confusion of others. If we don't look into hope and fear, seeing a thought arise, seeing the chain reaction that follows—if we don't train in sitting with that energy without getting snared by the drama, then we're always going to be afraid. The world we live in, the people we meet, the animals emerging from doorways—everything will become increasingly threatening.

So we start by simply looking into our own hearts and minds. Probably we start looking because we feel inadequate, or in pain, and want to clean up our act. But gradually our practice evolves. We start understanding that, just like us, other people also keep getting hooked by hope and fear. Everywhere we go, we see the misery that comes from buying into the eight worldly dharmas. It's also pretty obvious that people need help and that there's no way to benefit anybody unless we start with ourselves.

Our motivation for practicing begins to change, and we desire to become tamed and reasonable for the sake of other people. We still want to see how mind works and how we get seduced by samsara, but it's not just for ourselves. It's for our companions, our children, our bosses—it's for the whole human dilemma.

nine

six kinds of loneliness

Usually we regard loneliness as an enemy. Heartache is not
something we choose to invite in. It's restless and pregnant
and hot with the desire to escape and find something or
someone to keep us company. When we can rest in the
middle, we begin to have a nonthreatening relationship with
loneliness, a relaxing and cooling loneliness that completely
turns our usual fearful patterns upside down.

In the middle way, there is no reference point. The
mind with no reference point does not resolve itself,
does not fixate or grasp. How could we possibly have
no reference point? To have no reference point would
be to change a deep-seated habitual response to the
world: wanting to make it work out one way or the other.
If I can't go left or right, I will die! When we don't go left
or right, we feel like we are in a detox center. We're alone
cold turkey with all the edginess that we've been trying to
avoid by going left or right. That edginess can feel pretty
heavy.

However, years and years of going to the left or right, going to yes or no, going to right or wrong has never really changed anything. Scrambling for security has never brought anything but momentary joy. It's like changing the position of our legs in meditation. Our legs hurt from sitting cross-legged, so we move them. And then we feel, "Phew! What a relief!" But two and a half minutes later, we want to move them again. We keep moving around seeking pleasure, seeking comfort, and the satisfaction that we get is very short-lived.

We hear a lot about the pain of samsara, and we also hear about liberation. But we don't hear much about how painful it is to go from being completely stuck to becoming unstuck. The process of becoming unstuck requires tremendous bravery, because basically we are completely changing our way of perceiving reality, like changing our DNA. We are undoing a pattern that is not just our pattern. It's the human pattern: we project onto the world a zillion possibilities of attaining resolution. We can have whiter teeth, a weed-free lawn, a strife-free life, a world without embarrassment. We can live happily every after. This pattern keeps us dissatisfied and causes us a lot of suffering.

As human beings, not only do we seek resolution, but we also feel that we deserve resolution. However, not only do we not deserve resolution, we suffer from resolution. We don't deserve resolution; we deserve something better than that. We deserve our birthright, which is the middle way, an open state of mind that can relax with paradox and ambiguity. To the degree that we've been avoiding uncertainty, we're naturally going to have withdrawal symptoms—withdrawal from always thinking that there's a problem and that someone, somewhere, needs to fix it.

The middle way is wide open, but it's tough going, because it goes against the grain of an ancient neurotic pattern that we all share. When we feel lonely, when we feel hopeless, what we want to do is move to the right or the left. We don't want to sit and feel what we feel. We don't want to go through the detox. Yet the middle way encourages us to do just that. It encourages us to awaken the bravery that exists in everyone without exception, including you and me.

Meditation provides a way for us to train in the middle way—in staying right on the spot. We are encouraged not to judge whatever arises in our mind. In fact, we are encouraged not to even grasp whatever arises in our mind. What we usually call good or bad we simply acknowledge as thinking, without all the usual drama that goes along with right and wrong. We are instructed to let the thoughts come and go as if touching a bubble with a feather. This straightforward discipline prepares us to stop struggling and discover a fresh, unbiased state of being.

The experience of certain feelings can seem particularly pregnant with desire for resolution: loneliness, boredom, anxiety. Unless we can relax with these feelings, it's very hard to stay in the middle when we experience them. We want victory or defeat, praise or blame. For example, if somebody abandons us, we don't want to be with that raw discomfort. Instead, we conjure up a familiar identity of ourselves as a hapless victim. Or maybe we avoid the rawness by acting out and righteously telling the person how messed up he or she is. We automatically want to cover over the pain in one way or another, identifying with victory or victimhood.

Usually we regard loneliness as an enemy. Heartache is not something we choose to invite in. It's restless and pregnant and hot with the desire to escape and find something or someone to keep us company. When we can rest in the middle, we begin to have a nonthreatening relationship with loneliness, a relaxing and cooling loneliness that completely turns our usual fearful patterns upside down.

There are six ways of describing this kind of cool loneliness. They are: less desire, contentment, avoiding unnecessary activity, complete discipline, not wandering in the world of desire, and not seeking security from one's discursive thoughts.

Less desire is the willingness to be lonely without resolution when everything in us yearns for something to cheer us up and change our mood. Practicing this kind of loneliness is a way of sowing seeds so that fundamental restlessness decreases. In meditation, for example, every time we label "thinking" instead of getting endlessly run around by our thoughts, we are training in just being here without dissociation. We can't do that now to the degree that we weren't willing to do it yesterday or the day before or last week or last year. After we practice less desire wholeheartedly and consistently, something shifts. We feel less desire in the sense of being less solidly seduced by our Very Important Story Lines. So even if the hot loneliness is there, and for 1.6 seconds we sit with that restlessness when yesterday we couldn't sit for even one, that's the journey of the warrior. That's the path of bravery. The less we spin off and go crazy, the more we taste the satisfaction of cool loneliness. As the Zen master Katagiri Roshi often said, "One can be lonely and not be tossed away by it."

The second kind of loneliness is contentment. When we have nothing, we have nothing to lose. We don't have anything to lose but being programmed in our guts to feel that we have a lot to lose. Our feeling that we have a lot to lose is rooted in fear—of loneliness, of change, of anything that can't be resolved, of nonexistence. The hope that we can avoid this feeling and the fear that we can't become our reference point.

When we draw a line down the center of a page, we know who we are if we're on the right side and who we are if we're on the left side. But we don't know who we are when we don't put ourselves on either side. Then we just don't know what to do. We just don't know. We have no reference point, no hand to hold. At that point we can either freak out or settle in. Contentment is a synonym for loneliness, cool loneliness, settling down with cool loneliness. We give up believing that being able to escape our loneliness is going to bring any lasting happiness or joy or sense of well-being or courage or strength. Usually we have to give up this belief about a billion times, again and again making friends with our jumpiness and dread, doing the same old thing a billion times with awareness. Then without our even noticing, something begins to shift. We can just be lonely with no alternatives, content to be right here with the mood and texture of what's happening.

The third kind of loneliness is avoiding unnecesssary activities. When we're lonely in a "hot" way, we look for something to save us; we look for a way out. We get this queasy feeling that we call loneliness, and our minds just go wild trying to come up with companions to save us from despair. That's called unnecessary activity. It's a way of keeping ourselves busy so we don't have to feel any pain. It could take the form of obsessively daydreaming of true romance, or turning a tidbit of gossip into the six o'clock news, or even going off by ourselves into the wilderness. The point is that in all these activities, we are seeking companionship in our usual, habitual way, using our same old repetitive ways of distancing ourselves from the demon loneliness. Could we just settle down and have some compassion and respect for ourselves? Could we stop trying to escape from being alone with ourselves? What about practicing not jumping and grabbing when we begin to panic? Relaxing with loneliness is a worthy occupation. As the Japanese poet Ryokan says, "If you want to find the meaning, stop chasing after so many things."

Complete discipline is another component of cool loneliness. Complete discipline means that at every opportunity, we're willing to come back, just gently come back to the present moment. This is loneliness as complete discipline. We're willing to sit still, just be there, alone. We don't particularly have to cultivate this kind of loneliness; we could just sit still long enough to realize it's how things really are. We are fundamentally alone, and there is nothing anywhere to hold on to. Moreover, this is not a problem. In fact, it allows us to finally discover a competely unfabricated state of being. Our habitual assumptions—all our ideas about how things are—keep us from seeing anything in a fresh, open way. We say, "Oh yes, I know." But we don't know. We don't ultimately know anything. There's no certainty about anything. This basic truth hurts, and we want to run away from it. But coming back and relaxing with something as familiar as loneliness is good discipline for realizing the profundity of the unresolved moments of our lives. We are cheating ourselves when we run away from the ambiguity of loneliness.

Not wandering in the world of desire is another way of describing cool loneliness. Wandering in the world of *desire* involves looking for alternatives, seeking something to comfort us—food, drink, people. The word desire encompasses that addiction quality, the way we grab for something because we want to find a way to make things okay. That quality comes from never having grown up. We still want to go home and be able to open the refrigerator and find it full of our favorite goodies; when the going gets tough, we want to yell "Mom!" But what we're doing as we progress along the path is leaving home and becoming homeless. Not wandering in the world of desire is about relating directly with how things are. Loneliness is not a problem. Loneliness is nothing to be solved. The same is true for any other experience we might have.

Another aspect of cool loneliness is not seeking security from one's discursive thoughts. The rug's been pulled; the jig is up; there is no way to get out of this one! We don't even seek the companionship of our own constant conversation with ourselves about how it is and how it isn't, whether it is or whether it isn't, whether it should or whether it shouldn't, whether it can or whether it can't. With cool loneliness we do not expect security from our own internal chatter. That's why we are instructed to label it "thinking." It has no objective reality. It is transparent and ungraspable. We're encouraged to just touch that chatter and let it go, not make much ado about nothing.

Cool loneliness allows us to look honestly and without aggression at our own minds. We can gradually drop our ideals of who we think we ought to be, or who we think we want to be, or who we think other people think we want to be or ought to be. We give it up and just look directly with compassion and humor at who we are. Then loneliness is no threat and heartache, no punishment.

Cool loneliness doesn't provide any resolution or give us ground under our feet. It challenges us to step into a world of no reference point without polarizing or solidifying. This is called the middle way, or the sacred path of the warrior.

When you wake up in the morning and out of nowhere comes the heartache of alienation and loneliness, could you use that as a golden opportunity? Rather than persecuting yourself or feeling that something terribly wrong is happening, right there in the moment of sadness and longing, could you relax and touch the limitless space of the human heart? The next time you get a chance, experiment with this.

ten

curious about existence

Recognize impermanence and suffering and egolessness at
the kitchen-sink level, and be inquisitive about your reactions.
Find out for yourself about peace and whether or not it's
true that our fundamental situation is joyful.

There are three truths—traditionally called three
marks—of our existence: impermanence, suffering, and egolessness. Even though they accurately
describe the rock-bottom qualities of our existence, these
words sound threatening. It's easy to get the idea that
there is something wrong with impermanence, suffering,
and egolessness, which is like thinking that there is something wrong with our fundamental situation. But there's
nothing wrong with impermanence, suffering, and egolessness; they can be celebrated. Our fundamental situation is joyful.

Impermanence is the goodness of reality. Just as the
four seasons are in continual flux, winter changing to
spring to summer to autumn; just as day becomes night,

light becoming dark becoming light again—in the same way, everything is constantly evolving. Impermanence is the essence of everything. It is babies becoming children, then teenagers, then adults, then old people, and somewhere along the way dropping dead. Impermanence is meeting and parting. It's falling in love and falling out of love. Impermanence is bittersweet, like buying a new shirt and years later finding it as part of a patchwork quilt.

People have no respect for impermanence. We take no delight in it; in fact, we despair of it. We regard it as pain. We try to resist it by making things that will last—forever, we say—things that we don't have to wash, things that we don't have to iron. Somehow, in the process of trying to deny that things are always changing, we lose our sense of the sacredness of life. We tend to forget that we are part of the natural scheme of things.

Impermanence is a principle of harmony. When we don't struggle against it, we are in harmony with reality. Many cultures celebrate this connectedness. There are ceremonies marking all the transitions of life from birth to death, as well as meetings and partings, going into battle, losing the battle, and winning the battle. We too could acknowledge, respect, and celebrate impermanence.

But what about suffering? Why would we celebrate suffering? Doesn't that sound masochistic? Our suffering is based so much on our fear of impermanence. Our pain is so rooted in our one-sided, lopsided view of reality. Who ever got the idea that we could have pleasure without pain? It's promoted rather widely in this world, and we buy it. But pain and pleasure go together; they are inseparable. They can be celebrated. They are ordinary. Birth is painful and delightful. Death is painful and delight-ful. Everything that ends is also the beginning of something else. Pain is not a punishment; pleasure is not a reward.

Inspiration and wretchedness are inseparable. We always want to get rid of misery rather than see how it works together with joy. The point isn't to cultivate one thing as opposed to another, but to relate properly to where we are. Inspiration and wretchedness complement each other. With only inspiration, we become arrogant. With only wretchedness, we lose our vision. Feeling inspired cheers us up, makes us realize how vast and wonderful our world is. Feeling wretched humbles us. The gloriousness of our inspiration connects us with the sacredness of the world. But when the tables are turned and we feel wretched, that softens us up. It ripens our hearts. It becomes the ground for understanding others. Both the inspiration and the wretchedness can be celebrated. We can be big and small at the same time.

Can we also celebrate egolessness? Often we think of egolessness as a great loss, but actually it's a gain. The acknowledgment of egolessness, our natural state, is like regaining eyesight after having been blind or regaining hearing after having been deaf. Egolessness has been compared to the rays of the sun. With no solid sun, the rays just radiate outward. In the same way, wakefulness naturally radiates out when we're not so concerned with ourselves. Egolessness is the same thing as basic goodness or buddha nature, our unconditional being. It's what we always have and never really lose.

Ego could be defined as whatever covers up basic goodness. From an experiential point of view, what is ego covering up? It's covering up our experience of just being here, just fully being where we are, so that we can relate with the immediacy of our experience. Egolessness is a state of mind that has complete confidence in the sacredness of the world. It is unconditional well-being, unconditional joy that includes all the different qualities of our experience.

So how do we celebrate impermanence, suffering, and egolessness in our everyday lives? When impermanence presents itself in our lives, we can recognize it as impermanence. We don't have to look for opportunities to do this. When your pen runs out of ink in the middle of writing an important letter, recognize it as impermanence, part of the whole cycle of life. When someone's born, recognize it as impermanence. When someone dies, recognize it as impermanence. When your car gets stolen, recognize it as impermanence. When you fall in love, recognize it as impermanence, and let that intensify the preciousness. When a relationship ends, recognize it as impermanence. There are countless examples of impermanence in our lives every day, from the moment we wake up until we fall asleep and even while we're dreaming, all the time. This is a twenty-four-hour-a-day practice. Recognize impermanence as impermanence.

Then we can recognize our reaction to impermanence.

This is where curiosity comes in. Usually we just react habitually to events in our lives. We become resentful or delighted, excited or disappointed. There's no intelligence involved, no cheerfulness. But when we recognize impermanence as impermanence, we can also notice what our reaction to impermanence is. This is called mindfulness, awareness, curiosity, inquisitiveness, paying attention. Whatever we call it, it's a very helpful practice, the practice of coming to know ourselves completely.

When suffering arises in our lives, we can recognize it as suffering. When we get what we don't want, when we don't get what we do want, when we become ill, when we're getting old, when we're dying—when we see any of these things in our lives, we can recognize suffering as suffering. Then we can be curious, notice, and be mindful of our reactions to that. Again, usually we're either resentful and feel cheated somehow, or we're delighted. But whatever our reaction is, it's usually habitual. Instead, we could see the next impulse come up, and how we spin off from there. Spinning off is neither good nor bad; it's just something that happens as a reaction to the pleasure and pain of our existence. We can simply see that, without judgment or the intention to clean up our act.

When egolessness arises, we can recognize it as egolessness—a fresh moment, a clear perception of a smell or a sight or a sound, a feeling of opening to emotions or thoughts rather than closing off into our narrow limited selves. When we perceive the spaciousness in our lives, when we sense a gap in the continual conversation we have with ourselves, when we suddenly notice what's in front of us, when we take a fresh, clear, unedited look at reality, we can recognize it as egolessness. It doesn't have to be a big deal. Egolessness is available all the time as freshness, openness, delight in our sense perceptions. Curiously enough, we also experience egolessness when we don't know what's happening, when we've lost our reference point, when we get a shock and our mind is stopped. We can notice our reactions to that. Sometimes we open further; sometimes we quickly shut down. In any case, when egolessness occurs in our lives, we can recognize it as egolessness. We can notice, be curious, be mindful of our reactions and of what happens next.

Often peace is taught as the fourth mark of existence. This isn't the peace that's the opposite of war. It's the well-being that comes when we can see the infinite pairs of opposites as complementary. If there is beauty, there must be ugliness. If there is right, there is wrong. Wisdom and ignorance cannot be separated. This is an old truth—one that men and women like ourselves have been discovering for a long time. Cultivating moment-to-moment curiosity, we just might find that day by day this kind of peace dawns on us, and we begin to understand what all the books have been talking about.

So don't take anything for granted, and don't believe everything you're told. Without being cynical or gullible, look for the living quality of the dharma. Recognize impermanence and suffering and egolessness at the kitchen-sink level, and be inquisitive about your reactions. Find out for yourself about peace and whether or not it's true that our fundamental situation is joyful.

nonaggression and the four maras

All the maras point the way to being completely awake
and alive by letting go, by letting ourselves die moment after
moment, at the end of each out breath. When we wake up,
we can live fully without seeking pleasure and avoiding pain,
without re-creating ourselves when we fall apart.

On the night on which he was to attain enlightenment, the Buddha sat under a tree. While he was
sitting there, he was attacked by the forces of
Mara. The story goes that they shot swords and arrows at
him, and that their weapons turned into flowers.

What does this story mean? My understanding of it is
that what we habitually regard as obstacles are not really
our enemies, but rather our friends. What we call obstacles are really the way the world and our entire experience
teach us where we're stuck. What may appear to be an
arrow or a sword we can actually experience as a flower.
Whether we experience what happens to us as obstacle
and enemy or as teacher and friend depends entirely on

our perception of reality. It depends on our relationship with ourselves.

The teachings tell us that obstacles occur at the outer level and at the inner level. In this context, the outer level is the sense that something or somebody has harmed us, interfering with the harmony and peace we thought was ours. Some rascal has ruined it all. This particular sense of obstacle occurs in relationships and in many other situations; we feel disappointed, harmed, confused, and attacked in a variety of ways. People have felt this way from the beginning of time.

As for the inner level of obstacle, perhaps nothing ever really attacks us except our own confusion. Perhaps there is no solid obstacle except our own need to protect ourselves from being touched. Maybe the only enemy is that we don't like the way reality is *now* and therefore wish it would go away fast. But what we find as practitioners is that nothing ever goes away until it has taught us what we need to know. If we run a hundred miles an hour to the other end of the continent in order to get away from the obstacle, we find the very same problem waiting for us when we arrive. It just keeps returning with new names, forms, and manifestations until we learn whatever it has to teach us about where we are separating ourselves from reality, how we are pulling back instead of opening up, closing down instead of allowing ourselves to experience fully whatever we encounter, without hesitating or retreating into ourselves.

Trungpa Rinpoche once asked a group of students,

"What do you do when you get squeezed? What do you do when things are unbearable?" We all sat there, wondering what to say. Then he called on us one by one. We were so scared that we answered very genuinely. Almost all of us said something to the effect that we just completely fell apart, forgot about practice altogether, and became totally habitual in our reactions. Needless to say, after that we noticed very clearly what we did when we felt attacked, betrayed, or confused, when we found situations unbearable or unacceptable. We began to really notice what we did. Did we close down, or did we open up? Did we feel resentful and bitter, or did we soften? Did we become wiser or more stupid? As a result of our pain, did we know more about what it is to be human, or did we know less? Were we more critical of our world or more generous? Were we penetrated by the arrows, or did we turn them into flowers?

Traditional teachings on the forces of Mara describe the nature of obstacles and the nature of how human beings habitually become confused and lose confidence in our basic wisdom mind. The maras provide descriptions of some very familiar ways in which we try to avoid what is happening.

There are four maras. The first mara is called *devaputra mara*. It has to do with seeking pleasure. The second one, called *skandha mara*, has to do with how we always try to re-create ourselves, try to get some ground back, try to be who we think we are. The third mara is called *klesha mara*. It has to do with how we use our emotions to keep ourselves dumb or asleep. The fourth one, *yama mara*, has to do with the fear of death. The descriptions of these four maras show us four ways in which we, just like the Buddha, are seemingly attacked.

Devaputra mara involves seeking pleasure. It works like this: when we feel embarrassed or awkward, when pain presents itself to us in any form whatsoever, we run like crazy to try to become comfortable. Any obstacle we encounter has the power to completely pull the rug out, to completely pop the bubble of reality that we have come to regard as secure and certain. When we are threatened that way, we can't stand to feel the pain, the edginess, the anxiety, the queasiness in our stomach, the heat of anger rising, the bitter taste of resentment. Therefore, we try to grasp something pleasant. We react with this tragically human habit of seeking pleasure and trying to avoid pain.

The devaputra mara is a good description of how we are all addicted to avoiding pain. When pain arises, we reach again and again for something that will blot it out. Maybe we drink or take drugs or just chew gum or turn on the radio. We might even use meditation to try to escape from the more awkward, unpleasant, and penetrating aspects of being alive. Someone has just shot an arrow or raised a sword, and instead of allowing it to change into a flower, we run, trying to escape in all kinds of ways. There are, of course, endless ways of seeking pleasure and avoiding pain.

However, we don't have to consider seeking pleasure as an obstacle. Rather, seeking pleasure is an opportunity to observe what we do in the face of pain. Instead of trying to avoid our uneasiness and off-centeredness by running away, we could begin to open our hearts to the human dilemma that causes so much misery in this world. We could realize that the way to turn this devaputra arrow into a flower is to open our hearts and look at how we try to escape. With enormous gentleness and clarity, we could look at how weak we are. In this way we can discover that what seems to be ugly is in fact the source of wisdom and a way for us to reconnect with our basic wisdom mind.

Skandha mara is how we react when the rug is pulled out from under us. We feel that we have lost everything that's good. We've been thrown out of the nest. We sail through space without a clue as to what's going to happen next. We're in no-man's-land: we had it all together, working nicely, when suddenly the atomic bomb dropped and shattered our world into a million pieces. We don't know what's going to happen next or even where we are. Then we re-create ourselves. We return to the solid ground of our self-concept as quickly as possible. Trungpa Rinpoche used to call this "nostalgia for samsara."

Our whole world falls apart, and we've been given this great opportunity. However, we don't trust our basic wisdom mind enough to let it stay like that. Our habitual reaction is to want to get ourselves back—even our anger, resentment, fear, or bewilderment. So we re-create our solid, immovable personality as if we were Michelangelo chiseling ourselves out of marble.

Instead of a tragedy or melodrama, this mara is more

like a situation comedy. Just as we are on the verge of really understanding something, allowing our heart to truly open, just as we have the opportunity to see clearly, we put on a Groucho Marx mask with fluffy eyebrows and a big nose. Then we refuse to laugh or let go, because we might discover—who knows what?

Again, this process does not have to be considered an obstacle or a problem. Even though it feels like an arrow or a sword, if we use it as an opportunity to become aware of how we try to re-create ourselves over and over again, it turns into a flower. We can allow ourselves to be inquisitive or open about what has just happened and what will happen next. Instead of struggling to regain our concept of who we are, we can touch in to that mind of simply not knowing, which is basic wisdom mind.

The *klesha mara* is characterized by strong emotions. A simple feeling will arise, and instead of simply letting it be there, we panic. We begin to weave our thoughts into a story line, which gives rise to bigger emotions. Instead of just sitting in some kind of openness with our uncomfortable feeling, we bring out the bellows and fan away at it. With our thoughts and emotions, we keep it inflamed, hot; we won't let it go.

When everything falls apart and we feel uncertainty, disappointment, shock, embarrassment, what's left is a mind that is clear, unbiased, and fresh. But we don't see that. Instead, we feel the queasiness and uncertainty of being in no-man's-land and enlarge the feeling and march it down the street with banners that proclaim how bad everything is. We knock on every door asking people to sign petitions until there is a whole army of people who agree with us that everything is wrong. We forget what we've learned through meditation and know to be true. When really strong emotion comes up, all the doctrines and beliefs that we've held on to seem kind of pitiful by comparison, because emotions are so much more powerful.

So what began as an enormous open space becomes a forest fire, a world war, a volcano erupting, a tidal wave. We *use* our emotions. We *use* them. In their essence, they are simply part of the goodness of being alive, but instead of letting them be, we take them and use them to regain our ground. We use them to try to deny that in fact no one has ever known or will ever know what's happening. We use them to try to make everything secure and predictable and real again, to fool ourselves about what's really true. We could just sit with the emotional energy and let it pass. There's no particular need to spread blame and self-justification. Instead, we throw kerosene on the emotion so it will feel more real.

Again, we do not have to consider this process an obstacle or a problem. If we can look at and see the wildness of emotion, we can not only begin to befriend and soften toward ourselves, but we can also begin to befriend all human beings and indeed all living beings. By becoming aware of how we do this silly thing again and again because we don't want to dwell in the uncertainty and awkwardness and pain of not knowing, we begin to develop true compassion for ourselves and everyone else, because we see what happens and how we react when things fall apart. That awareness is what turns the sword into a flower. It is how what is seemingly ugly and problematic and unwanted actually becomes our teacher.

I think maybe all of the maras arise from fear of death, but *yama mara* is particularly rooted there. When we talk about a good life from the usual samsaric point of view, what we mean is that we've finally gotten it together. We finally feel that we're a good person. We have good qualities, we're peaceful, and we don't get thrown off balance when arrows are shot at us. We're the person who knows how to turn an arrow into a flower. We feel so good about ourselves. We've finally tied up all the loose ends. We're happy. We think that that's life.

We think that if we just meditated enough or jogged enough or ate perfect food, everything would be perfect. But from the point of view of someone who is awake, that's death. Seeking security or perfection, rejoicing in feeling confirmed and whole, self-contained and comfortable, is some kind of death. It doesn't have any fresh air. There's no room for something to come in and interrupt all that. We are killing the moment by controlling our experience. Doing this is setting ourselves up for failure, because sooner or later, we're going to have an experience we can't control: our house is going to burn down, someone we love is going to die, we're going to find out we have cancer, a brick is going to fall out of the sky and hit us on the head, somebody's going to spill tomato juice all over our white suit, or we're going to arrive at our favorite restaurant and discover that no one ordered produce and seven hundred people are coming for lunch.

The essence of life is that it's challenging. Sometimes it is sweet, and sometimes it is bitter. Sometimes your body tenses, and sometimes it relaxes or opens. Sometimes you have a headache, and sometimes you feel 100 percent healthy. From an awakened perspective, trying to tie up all the loose ends and finally get it together is death, because it involves rejecting a lot of your basic experience. There is something aggressive about that approach to life, trying to flatten out all the rough spots and imperfections into a nice smooth ride.

To be fully alive, fully human, and completely awake is to be continually thrown out of the nest. To live fully is to be always in no-man's-land, to experience each moment as completely new and fresh. To live is to be willing to die over and over again. From the awakened point of view, that's life. Death is wanting to hold on to what you have and to have every experience confirm you and congratulate you and make you feel completely together. So even though we say the yama mara is fear of death, it's actually fear of life.

We want to be perfect, but we just keep seeing our imperfections, and there is no room to get away from that, no exit, nowhere to run. That is when this sword turns into a flower. We stick with what we see, we feel what we feel, and from that we begin to connect with our own wisdom mind.

Without the maras, would the Buddha have awakened?

Would he have attained enlightenment without them? Weren't they his best friends, since they showed him who he was and what was true? All the maras point the way to being completely awake and alive by letting go, by letting ourselves die moment after moment, at the end of each out-breath. When we wake up, we can live fully without seeking pleasure and avoiding pain, without re-creating ourselves when we fall apart. We can let ourselves feel our emotions as hot or cold, vibrating or smooth, instead of using our emotions to keep ourselves ignorant and dumb. We can give up on being perfect and experience each moment to its fullest. Trying to run away is never the answer to being a fully human being. Running away from the immediacy of our experience is like preferring death to life.

Looking at the arrows and swords, and how we react to them, we can always return to basic wisdom mind. Rather than trying to get rid of something or buying into a dualistic sense of being attacked, we take the opportunity to see how we close down when we're squeezed. This is how we open our hearts. It is how we awaken our intelligence and connect with fundamental buddha nature.

twelve

growing up

From the very beginning to the very end, pointing to our own hearts to discover what is true isn't just a matter of honesty but also of compassion and respect for what we see.

In my office there is a scroll with Japanese calligraphy and a painting of Zen master Bodhidharma. Bodhidharma is a fat, grumpy-looking man with bushy eyebrows. He looks as if he has indigestion. The calligraphy reads, "Pointing directly at your own heart, you find Buddha."

Listening to talks about the dharma, or the teachings of Buddha, or practicing meditation is nothing other than studying ourselves. Whether we're eating or working or meditating or listening or talking, the reason that we're here in this world at all is to study ourselves. In fact, it has been said that studying ourselves provides all the books we need.

Maybe the reason there are dharma talks and books is just to encourage us to understand this simple teaching: all the wisdom about how we cause ourselves to suffer and all the wisdom about how joyful and vast and uncomplicated our minds are—these two things, the understanding of what we might call neurosis and the wisdom of unconditioned, unbiased truth—can only be found in our own experience.

Bodhidharma brought Zen Buddhism from India to China. He was well known for being fierce and uncompromising. There is a story about how he kept nodding off during meditation, so he cut off his eyelids. When he threw them on the ground, they turned into a tea plant, and then he realized he could simply drink the tea to stay awake! He was uncompromising in that he wanted to know what was true, and he wasn't going to take anybody else's word for it. His big discovery was that by looking directly into our own heart, we find the awakened Buddha, the completely unclouded experience of how things really are.

In all kinds of situations, we can find out what is true simply by studying ourselves in every nook and cranny, in every black hole and bright spot, whether it's murky, creepy, grisly, splendid, spooky, frightening, joyful, inspiring, peaceful, or wrathful. We can just look at the whole thing. There's a lot of encouragement to do this, and meditation gives us the method. When I first encountered Buddhism, I was extremely relieved that there were not only teachings, but also a technique I could use to explore and test these teachings. I was told from day one that, just like Bodhidharma, I had to find out for myself what was true.

However, when we sit down to meditate and take an honest look at our minds, there is a tendency for it to become a rather morbid and depressing project. We can lose all sense of humor and sit with the grim determination to get to the bottom of this stinking mess. After a while, when people have been practicing that way, they begin to feel so much guilt and distress that they just break down, and they might say to someone they trust, "Where's the *joy* in all this?"

So, along with clear seeing, there's another important element, and that's kindness. It seems that, without clarity and honesty, we don't progress. We just stay stuck in the same vicious cycle. But honesty without kindness makes us feel grim and mean, and pretty soon we start looking like we've been sucking on lemons. We become so caught up in introspection that we lose any contentment or gratitude we might have had. The sense of being irritated by ourselves and our lives and other people's idiosyncrasies becomes overwhelming. That's why there's so much emphasis on kindness.

Sometimes it's expressed as heart, awakening your heart. Often it's called gentleness. Sometimes it's called unlimited friendliness. But basically kindness is a down-to-earth, everyday way to describe the important ingredient that balances out the whole picture and helps us connect with unconditional joy. As the Vietnamese teacher Thich Nhat Hanh says, "Suffering is not enough."

Discipline is important. When we sit down to meditate, we are encouraged to stick with the technique and be faithful to the instructions, but within that container of discipline, why do we have to be so harsh? Do we meditate because we "should"? Do we do it to become "good" Buddhists, to please our teacher, or to escape going to hell? How we regard what arises in meditation is training for how we regard whatever arises in the rest of our lives. So the challenge is how to develop compassion right along with clear seeing, how to train in lightening up and cheering up rather than becoming more guilt-ridden and miserable. Otherwise, all that happens is that we all cut everybody else down, and we also cut ourselves down. Nothing ever measures up. Nothing is ever good enough. Honesty without kindness, humor, and goodheartedness can be just mean. From the very beginning to the very end, pointing to our own hearts to discover what is true isn't just a matter of honesty but also of compassion and respect for what we see.

Learning how to be kind to ourselves, learning how to respect ourselves, is important. The reason it's important is that, fundamentally, when we look into our own hearts and begin to discover what is confused and what is brilliant, what is bitter and what is sweet, it isn't just ourselves that we're discovering. We're discovering the universe. When we discover the Buddha that we are, we realize that everything and everyone is Buddha. We discover that everything is awake, and everyone is awake. Everything is equally precious and whole and good, and everyone is equally precious and whole and good. When we regard thoughts and emotions with humor and openness, that's how we perceive the universe. We're not just talking about our individual liberation, but how to help the community we live in, how to help our families, our country, and the whole continent, not to mention the world and the galaxy and as far as we want to go.

There's an interesting transition that occurs naturally and spontaneously. We begin to find that, to the degree that there is bravery in ourselves—the willingness to look, to point directly at our own hearts—and to the degree that there is kindness toward ourselves, there is confidence that we can actually forget ourselves and open to the world.

The only reason that we don't open our hearts and minds to other people is that they trigger confusion in us that we don't feel brave enough or sane enough to deal with. To the degree that we look clearly and compassionately at ourselves, we feel confident and fearless about looking into someone else's eyes.

Then this experience of opening to the world begins to benefit ourselves and others simultaneously. The more we relate with others, the more quickly we discover where we are blocked, where we are unkind, afraid, shut down. Seeing this is helpful, but it is also painful. Often the only way we know how to react is to use it as ammunition against ourselves. We aren't kind. We aren't honest. We aren't brave, and we might as well give up right now. But when we apply the instruction to be soft and nonjudgmental to whatever we see right at that very moment, then this embarrassing reflection in the mirror becomes our friend. Seeing that reflection becomes motivation to soften further and lighten up more, because we know it's the only way we can continue to work with others and be of any benefit to the world.

That's the beginning of growing up. As long as we don't want to be honest and kind with ourselves, then we are always going to be infants. When we begin just to try to accept ourselves, the ancient burden of self-importance lightens up considerably. Finally there's room for genuine inquisitiveness, and we find we have an appetite for what's out there.

thirteen

widening the circle
of compassion

> Only in an open, nonjudgmental space can we
> acknowledge what we are feeling. Only in an open
> space where we're not all caught up in our own
> version of reality can we see and hear and feel who
> others really are, which allows us to be with them
> and communicate with them properly.

When we talk of compassion, we usually mean working with those less fortunate than ourselves. Because we have better opportunities, a good education, and good health, we should be compassionate toward those poor people who don't have any of that. However, in working with the teachings on how to awaken compassion and in trying to help others, we might come to realize that compassionate action involves working with ourselves as much as working with others. Compassionate action is a practice, one of the most advanced. There's nothing more advanced than relating with others. There's nothing more advanced than communication—compassionate communication.

To relate with others compassionately is a challenge. Really communicating to the heart and being there for someone else—our child, spouse, parent, client, patient, or the homeless woman on the street—means not shutting down on that person, which means, first of all, not shutting down on ourselves. This means allowing ourselves to feel what we feel and not pushing it away. It means accepting every aspect of ourselves, even the parts we don't like. To do this requires openness, which in Buddhism is sometimes called emptiness—not fixating or holding on to anything. Only in an open, nonjudgmental space can we acknowledge what we are feeling. Only in an open space where we're not all caught up in our own version of reality can we see and hear and feel who others really are, which allows us to be with them and communicate with them properly.

Recently I was talking with an old man who has been living on the streets for the last four years. Nobody ever looks at him. No one ever talks to him. Maybe somebody gives him a little money, but nobody ever looks in his face and asks him how he's doing. The feeling that he doesn't exist for other people, the sense of loneliness and isolation, is intense. He reminded me that the essence of compassionate speech or compassionate action is to be there for people, without pulling back in horror or fear or anger.

Being compassionate is a pretty tall order. All of us are in relationships every day of our lives, but particularly if we are people who want to help others—people with cancer, people with AIDS, abused women or children, abused animals, anyone who's hurting—something we soon notice is that the person we set out to help may trigger unresolved issues in us. Even though we want to help, and maybe we do help for a few days or a month or two, sooner or later someone walks through that door and pushes all our buttons. We find ourselves hating those people or scared of them or feeling like we just can't handle them. This is true always, if we are sincere about wanting to benefit others. Sooner or later, all our own unresolved issues will come up; we'll be confronted with ourselves.

Roshi Bernard Glassman is a Zen teacher who runs a project for the homeless in Yonkers, New York. Last time I heard him speak, he said something that struck me: he said he doesn't really do this work to help others; he does it because he feels that moving into the areas of society that he had rejected is the same as working with the parts of himself that he had rejected.

Although this is ordinary Buddhist thinking, it's difficult to live it. It's even difficult to hear that what we reject out there is what we reject in ourselves, and what we reject in ourselves is what we are going to reject out there. But that, in a nutshell, is how it works. If we find ourselves unworkable and give up on ourselves, then we'll find others unworkable and give up on them. What we hate in ourselves, we'll hate in others. To the degree that we have compassion for ourselves, we will also have compassion for others. Having compassion starts and ends with having compassion for all those unwanted parts of ourselves, all those imperfections that we don't even want to look at. Compassion isn't some kind of self-improvement project or ideal that we're trying to live up to.

There's a slogan in the mahayana* teachings that says, "Drive all blames into oneself." The essence of this slogan is, "When it hurts so bad, it's because I am hanging on so tight." It's not saying that we should beat ourselves up. It's not advocating martyrdom. What it implies is that pain comes from holding so tightly to having it our own way and that one of the main exits we take when we find ourselves uncomfortable, when we find ourselves in an unwanted situation or an unwanted place, is to blame.

We habitually erect a barrier called blame that keeps us from communicating genuinely with others, and we fortify it with our concepts of who's right and who's wrong. We do that with the people who are closest to us, and we do it with political systems, with all kinds of things that we don't like about our associates or our society. It is a very common, ancient, well-perfected device for trying to feel better. Blame others. Blaming is a way to protect our hearts, to try to protect what is soft and open and tender in ourselves. Rather than own that pain, we scramble to find some comfortable ground.

This slogan is a helpful and interesting suggestion that we could begin to shift that deep-seated, ancient, habitual tendency to hang on to having everything on our own

* The "great vehicle," which presents vision based on emptiness, compassion, and acknowledgment of universal buddha nature.

terms. The way to start would be, first, when we feel the tendency to blame, to try to get in touch with what it feels like to be holding on to ourselves so tightly. What does it feel like to blame? How does it feel to reject? What does it feel like to hate? What does it feel like to be righteously indignant?

In each of us, there's a lot of softness, a lot of heart. Touching that soft spot has to be the starting place. This is what compassion is all about. When we stop blaming long enough to give ourselves an open space in which to feel our soft spot, it's as if we're reaching down to touch a large wound that lies right underneath the protective shell that blaming builds.

Buddhist words such as *compassion* and *emptiness* don't mean much until we start cultivating our innate ability simply to be there with pain with an open heart and the willingness not to instantly try to get ground under our feet. For instance, if what we're feeling is rage, we usually assume that there are only two ways to relate to it. One is to blame others. Lay it all on somebody else; drive all blames into everyone else. The other alternative is to feel guilty about our rage and blame ourselves.

Blame is a way in which we solidify ourselves. Not only do we point the finger when something is "wrong," but we also want to make things "right." In any relationship that we stick with, be it marriage or parenthood, employment, a spiritual community, or whatever, we may also find that we want to make it "righter" than it is, because we're a little nervous. Maybe it isn't exactly living up to our standards, so we justify it and justify it and try to make it extremely right. We tell everybody that our husband or wife or child or teacher or support group is doing some sort of peculiar antisocial thing for good spiritual reasons. Or we come up with some dogmatic belief and hold on to it with a vengeance, again to solidify our ground. We have some sense that we have to make things right according to our standards. If we just can't stick with a situation any longer, then it goes over the edge and we make it wrong because we think that's our only alternative. Something's right or something's wrong.

We start with ourselves. We make ourselves right or we make ourselves wrong, every day, every week, every month and year of our lives. We feel that we have to be right so that we can feel good. We don't want to be wrong because then we'll feel bad. But we could be more compassionate toward all these parts of ourselves. When we feel right, we can look at that. Feeling right can feel good; we can be completely sure of how right we are and have a lot of people agreeing with us about how right we are. But suppose someone does not agree with us? Then what happens? Do we find ourselves getting angry and aggressive? If we look into the very moment of anger or aggression, we might see that this is what wars are made of. This is what race riots are made of: feeling that we have to be right, being thrown off and righteously indignant when someone disagrees with us. On the other hand, when we find ourselves feeling wrong, convinced that we're wrong, getting solid about being wrong, we could also look at that. The whole right and wrong business closes us down and makes our world smaller. Wanting situations and relationships to be solid, permanent, and graspable obscures the pith of the matter, which is that things are fundamentally groundless.

Instead of making others right or wrong, or bottling up right and wrong in ourselves, there's a middle way, a very powerful middle way. We could see it as sitting on the razor's edge, not falling off to the right or the left. This middle way involves not hanging on to our version so tightly. It involves keeping our hearts and minds open long enough to entertain the idea that when we make things wrong, we do it out of a desire to obtain some kind of ground or security. Equally, when we make things right, we are still trying to obtain some kind of ground or security. Could our minds and our hearts be big enough just to hang out in that space where we're not entirely certain about who's right and who's wrong? Could we have no agenda when we walk into a room with another person, not know what to say, not make that person wrong or right? Could we see, hear, feel other people as they really are? It is powerful to practice this way, because we'll find ourselves continually rushing around to try to feel secure again—to make ourselves or them either right or wrong. But true communication can happen only in that open space.

Whether it's ourselves, our lovers, bosses, children, local Scrooge, or the political situation, it's more daring and real not to shut anyone out of our hearts and not to make the other into an enemy. If we begin to live like this, we'll find that we actually can't make things completely right or completely wrong anymore, because things are a lot more slippery and playful than that. Everything is ambiguous; everything is always shifting and changing, and there are as many different takes on any given situation as there are people involved. Trying to find absolute rights and wrongs is a trick we play on ourselves to feel secure and comfortable.

This leads to a bigger underlying issue for all of us: How are we ever going to change anything? How is there going to be less aggression in the universe rather than more? We can then bring it down to a more personal level: how do I learn to communicate with somebody who is hurting me or someone who is hurting a lot of people? How do I speak to someone so that some change actually occurs? How do I communicate so that the space opens up and both of us begin to touch in to some kind of basic intelligence that we all share? In a potentially violent encounter, how do I communicate so that neither of us becomes increasingly furious and aggressive? How do I communicate to the heart so that a stuck situation can ventilate? How do I communicate so that things that seem frozen, unworkable, and eternally aggressive begin to soften up, and some kind of compassionate exchange begins to happen?

Well, it starts with being willing to feel what we are going through. It starts with being willing to have a compassionate relationship with the parts of ourselves that we feel are not worthy of existing on the planet. If we are willing through meditation to be mindful not only of what feels comfortable, but also of what pain feels like, if we even *aspire* to stay awake and open to what we're feeling, to recognize and acknowledge it as best we can in each moment, then something begins to change.

Compassionate action, being there for others, being able to act and speak in a way that communicates, starts with seeing ourselves when we start to make ourselves right or make ourselves wrong. At that particular point, we could just contemplate the fact that there is a larger alternative to either of those, a more tender, shaky kind of place where we could live. This place, if we can touch it, will help us train ourselves throughout our lives to open further to whatever we feel, to open further rather than shut down more. We'll find that as we begin to commit ourselves to this practice, as we begin to have a sense of celebrating the aspects of ourselves that we found so impossible before, something will shift in us. Something will shift permanently in us. Our ancient habitual patterns will begin to soften, and we'll begin to see the faces and hear the words of people who are talking to us.

If we begin to get in touch with whatever we feel with some kind of kindness, our protective shells will melt, and we'll find that more areas of our lives are workable. As we learn to have compassion for ourselves, the circle of compassion for others—what and whom we can work with, and how—becomes wider.

fourteen

the love that
will not die

In difficult times, it is only bodhichitta that heals. When
inspiration has become hidden, when we feel ready to
give up, this is the time when healing can be found in the
tenderness of pain itself. This is the time to touch the
genuine heart of bodhichitta.

The father of a two-year-old talks about turning
on the television and unexpectedly seeing the
bombing of the federal building in Oklahoma City.
He watched as the firemen carried the limp and bloody
bodies of toddlers from the ruins of the day-care center on
the building's first floor. He says that in the past he was
able to distance himself from other people's suffering. But
since he's become a father, things have changed. He feels
as if each of those children were his child. He feels the
grief of all the parents as his own grief.

This kinship with the suffering of others, this inability
to continue to regard it from afar, is the discovery of our
soft spot, the discovery of *bodhichitta*. *Bodhichitta* is a

Sanskrit word that means "noble or awakened heart." It is said to be present in all beings. Just as butter is inherent in milk and oil is inherent in a sesame seed, this soft spot is inherent in you and me.

Stephen Levine writes of a woman who was dying in terrible pain and feeling overwhelming bitterness. At the point at which she felt she couldn't bear the suffering and resentment any longer, she unexpectedly began to experience the pain of others in agony: a starving mother in Ethiopia, a runaway teenager dying of an overdose in a dirty flat, a man crushed by a landslide and dying alone by the banks of a river. She said she understood that it wasn't her pain, it was the pain of all beings. It wasn't just her life, it was life itself.

We awaken this bodhichitta, this tenderness for life, when we can no longer shield ourselves from the vulnerability of our condition, from the basic fragility of existence. In the words of the sixteenth Gyalwa Karmapa, "You take it all in. You let the pain of the world touch your heart and you turn it into compassion."

It is said that in difficult times, it is only bodhichitta that heals. When inspiration has become hidden, when we feel ready to give up, this is the time when healing can be found in the tenderness of pain itself. This is the time to touch the genuine heart of bodhichitta. In the midst of loneliness, in the midst of fear, in the middle of feeling misunderstood and rejected is the heartbeat of all things, the genuine heart of sadness.

Just as a jewel that has been buried in the earth for a

million years is not discolored or harmed, in the same way this noble heart is not affected by all of our kicking and screaming. The jewel can be brought out into the light at any time, and it will glow as brilliantly as if nothing had ever happened. No matter how committed we are to unkindness, selfishness, or greed, the genuine heart of bodhichitta cannot be lost. It is here in all that lives, never marred and completely whole.

We think that by protecting ourselves from suffering we are being kind to ourselves. The truth is, we only become more fearful, more hardened, and more alienated. We experience ourselves as being separate from the whole. This separateness becomes like a prison for us, a prison that restricts us to our personal hopes and fears and to caring only for the people nearest to us. Curiously enough, if we primarily try to shield ourselves from discomfort, we suffer. Yet when we don't close off and we let our hearts break, we discover our kinship with all beings. His Holiness the Dalai Lama describes two kinds of selfish people: the unwise and the wise. Unwise selfish people think only of themselves, and the result is confusion and pain. Wise selfish people know that the best thing they can do for themselves is to be there for others. As a result, they experience joy.

When we see a woman and her child begging on the street, when we see a man mercilessly beating his terrified dog, when we see a teenager who has been badly beaten or see fear in the eyes of a child, do we turn away because we can't bear it? Most of us probably do. Someone needs to encourage us not to brush aside what we feel, not to be ashamed of the love and grief it arouses in us, not to be afraid of pain. Someone needs to encourage us that this soft spot in us could be awakened and that to do this would change our lives.

The practice of *tonglen*—sending and receiving—is designed to awaken bodhichitta, to put us in touch with genuine noble heart. It is a practice of taking in pain and sending out pleasure and therefore completely turns around our well-established habit of doing just the opposite.

Tonglen is a practice of creating space, ventilating the atmosphere of our lives so that people can breathe freely and relax. Whenever we encounter suffering in any form, the tonglen instruction is to breathe it in with the wish that everyone could be free of pain. Whenever we encounter happiness in any form, the instruction is to breathe it out, send it out, with the wish that everyone could feel joy. It's a practice that allows people to feel less burdened and less cramped, a practice that shows us how to love without conditions.

Bo and Sita Lozoff have been helping people in prison for over twenty years. They teach meditation, they give talks, and in books and newsletters they give earthy and inspiring spiritual advice. Every day their mailbox is packed with letters from people doing time. Every day they answer as many as they can. Sita told me that sometimes those letters would be so filled with misery that she would feel overwhelmed. Then, without ever having heard of tonglen, she just naturally began breathing in all the pain in those letters and sending out relief.

Many people who are dying of AIDS have begun to do tonglen. They breathe in for all the others in the same boat. They breathe in the suffering of millions of men, women, and children who have AIDS. They breathe out a wellness, a kindness. As one man said, "It doesn't hurt me. It makes me feel that my pain is not in vain, that I am not alone and useless. It makes all of this worthwhile."

When we protect ourselves so we won't feel pain, that protection becomes like armor, like armor that imprisons the softness of the heart. We do everything we can think of not to feel anything threatening. We try to prolong feeling good about ourselves. Looking at color pictures in magazines of people having fun on the beach, many of us earnestly wish that life could be that good.

When we breathe in pain, somehow it penetrates that armor. The way we guard ourselves is getting softened up. This heavy, rusty, creaking armor begins to seem not so monolithic after all. With the in-breath the armor begins to fall apart, and we find we can breathe deeply and relax. A kindness and a tenderness begin to emerge. We don't have to tense up as if our whole life were being spent in the dentist's chair.

When we breathe out relief and spaciousness, we are also encouraging the armor to dissolve. The out-breath is a metaphor for opening our whole being. When something is precious, instead of holding it tightly, we can open our hands and share it. We can give it all away.

We can share the wealth of this unfathomable human experience.

A man who had been sexually abused as a baby begins to have complete recall. Without knowing where the inspiration comes from, he begins to breathe in all the pain of that terrified and helpless infant. Then he breathes in the pain of all babies everywhere, babies who are just barely surviving because of neglect, abuse, disease, and war. Out of nowhere, he discovers bodhichitta.

Awakened heart can always be discovered like that. It does not take gearing up or struggling to achieve. When strategies are not yet formed and we feel uncertain about which way to turn, in those moments of vulnerability, bodhichitta is always there. It manifests as basic openness, which Buddhists call *shunyata*. It manifests as basic tenderness, basic compassionate warmth. When we walk around like we're expecting to be attacked, we block it. When we release the tension between this and that, the struggle between us and them, that's when bodhichitta will emerge.

At the relative level, our noble heart is felt as kinship with all beings. At the absolute level, we experience it as groundlessness or open space.

Because bodhichitta gives us no ground, it cuts through our concepts and ideals. We can't make it into a project of becoming a "good person" or the one you can always count on to be there. It's far more uncertain than that.

Because bodhichitta awakens tenderness, we can't use it to distance ourselves. Bodhichitta can't be reduced to an abstraction about the emptiness of pain. We can't get away with saying, "There is nothing happening and nothing to do."

The relative and absolute work together to connect us with unlimited love. Compassion and shunyata are the qualities of a love that will not die.

When we experience the soft spot of bodhichitta, it's like returning home. It's as if we had amnesia for a very long time and awaken to remember who we really are. The poet Jalaluddin Rumi writes of night travelers who search the darkness instead of running from it, a companionship of people willing to know their own fear. Whether it's in the small fears of a job interview or the unnameable terrors imposed by war, prejudice, and hatred; whether it's in the loneliness of a widow or the horrors of children shamed or abused by a parent, in the tenderness of the pain itself, night travelers discover the light of bodhichitta.

Bodhichitta is available in moments of caring for things, when we clean our glasses or brush our hair. It's available in moments of appreciation, when we notice the blue sky or pause and listen to the rain. It is available in moments of gratitude, when we recall a kindness or recognize another person's courage. It is available in music and dance, in art, and in poetry. Whenever we let go of holding on to ourselves and look at the world around us, whenever we connect with sorrow, whenever we connect with joy, whenever we drop our resentment and complaint, in those moments bodhichitta is here.

Spiritual awakening is frequently described as a journey to the top of a mountain. We leave our attachments and our worldliness behind and slowly make our way to the top. At the peak we have transcended all pain. The only problem with this metaphor is that we leave all the others behind—our drunken brother, our schizophrenic sister, our tormented animals and friends. Their suffering continues, unrelieved by our personal escape.

In the process of discovering bodhichitta, the journey goes down, not up. It's as if the mountain pointed toward the center of the earth instead of reaching into the sky. Instead of transcending the suffering of all creatures, we move toward the turbulence and doubt. We jump into it. We slide into it. We tiptoe into it. We move toward it however we can. We explore the reality and unpredictability of insecurity and pain, and we try not to push it away. If it takes years, if it takes lifetimes, we let it be as it is. At our own pace, without speed or aggression, we move down and down and down. With us move millions of others, our companions in awakening from fear. At the bottom we discover water, the healing water of bodhichitta. Right down there in the thick of things, we discover the love that will not die.

fifteen

going against
the grain

Tonglen reverses the usual logic of avoiding suffering and
seeking pleasure. In the process, we become liberated from
very ancient patterns of selfishness. We begin to feel love
for both ourselves and others; we begin to take care of
ourselves and others. Tonglen awakens our compassion
and introduces us to a far bigger view of reality.

In order to feel compassion for other people, we have
to feel compassion for ourselves. In particular, to care
about people who are fearful, angry, jealous, overpow-
ered by addictions of all kinds, arrogant, proud, miserly,
selfish, mean, you name it—to have compassion and to
care for these people means not to run from the pain
of finding these things in ourselves. In fact, our whole
attitude toward pain can change. Instead of fending it
off and hiding from it, we could open our hearts and
allow ourselves to feel that pain, feel it as something that
will soften and purify us and make us far more loving
and kind.

Tonglen practice is a method for connecting with suffering—our own and that which is all around us, everywhere we go. It is a method for overcoming our fear of suffering and for dissolving the tightness of our hearts. Primarily it is a method for awakening the compassion that is inherent in all of us, no matter how cruel or cold we might seem to be.

We begin the practice by taking on the suffering of a person whom we know to be hurting and wish to help. For instance, if we know of a child who is being hurt, we breathe in with the wish to take away all of that child's pain and fear. Then, as we breathe out, we send happiness, joy, or whatever would relieve the child. This is the core of the practice: breathing in others' pain so they can be well and have more space to relax and open— breathing out, sending them relaxation or whatever we feel would bring them relief and happiness.

Often, however, we can't do this practice because we come face to face with our own fear, our own resistance or anger, or whatever our personal pain happens to be just then.

At that point we can change the focus and begin to do tonglen for what we are feeling and for millions of other people just like us who at that very moment are feeling exactly the same stuckness and misery. Maybe we are able to name our pain. We recognize it clearly as terror or revulsion or anger or wanting to get revenge. So we breathe in for all the people who are caught with that same emotion, and we send out relief or whatever opens up the space for ourselves and all those countless others. Maybe we can't name what we're feeling. But we can feel it—a tightness in the stomach, a heavy darkness, or whatever. We simply contact what we are feeling and breathe in, take it *in*, for all of us—and send *out* relief to all of us.

People often say that this practice goes against the grain of how we usually hold ourselves together. Truthfully, this practice *does* go against the grain of wanting things on our own terms, wanting everything to work out for ourselves no matter what happens to the others. The practice dissolves the walls we've built around our hearts. It dissolves the layers of self-protection we've tried so hard to create. In Buddhist language, one would say that it dissolves the fixation and clinging of ego.

Tonglen reverses the usual logic of avoiding suffering and seeking pleasure. In the process, we become liberated from very ancient patterns of selfishness. We begin to feel love for both ourselves and others; we begin to take care of ourselves and others. Tonglen awakens our compassion and introduces us to a far bigger view of reality. It introduces us to the unlimited spaciousness of shunyata. By doing the practice, we begin to connect with the open dimension of our being. At first this allows us to experience things as not such a big deal and not so solid as they seemed before.

Tonglen can be done for those who are ill, those who are dying or have died, those who are in pain of any kind. It can be done as a formal meditation practice or right on the spot at any time. We are out walking and we see someone in pain—right on the spot we can begin to breathe in that person's pain and send out relief. Or we are just as likely to see someone in pain and look away. The pain brings up our fear or anger; it brings up our resistance and confusion. So on the spot we can do tonglen for all the people just like ourselves, all those who wish to be compassionate but instead are afraid—who wish to be brave but instead are cowardly. Rather than beating ourselves up, we can use our personal stuckness as a stepping stone to understanding what people are up against all over the world. Breathe in for all of us and breathe out for all of us. Use what seems like poison as medicine. We can use our personal suffering as the path to compassion for all beings.

When you do tonglen on the spot, simply breathe in and breathe out, taking in pain and sending out spaciousness and relief.

When you do tonglen as a formal meditation practice, it has four stages:

1. First, rest your mind briefly, for a second or two, in a state of openness or stillness. This stage is traditionally called flashing on absolute bodhichitta, or suddenly opening to basic spaciousness and clarity.
2. Second, work with texture. Breathe in a feeling of hot, dark, and heavy—a sense of claustrophobia—and breathe out a feeling of cool, bright, and light—a sense of freshness. Breathe in completely, through all the pores of your body, and breathe out, radiate out,

completely, through all the pores of your body. Do this until it feels synchronized with your in- and out-breaths.

3. Third, work with a personal situation—any painful situation that's real to you. Traditionally you begin by doing tonglen for someone you care about and wish to help. However, as I described, if you are stuck, you can do the practice for the pain you are feeling and simultaneously for all those just like you who feel that kind of suffering. For instance, if you are feeling inadequate, you breathe that in for yourself and all the others in the same boat, and you send out confidence and adequacy or relief in any form you wish.

4. Finally, make the taking in and sending out bigger. If you are doing tonglen for someone you love, extend it out to those who are in the same situation as your friend. If you are doing tonglen for someone you see on television or on the street, do it for all the others in the same boat. Make it bigger than just that one person. If you are doing tonglen for all those who are feeling the anger or fear or whatever that you are trapped in, maybe that's big enough. But you could go further in all these cases. You could do tonglen for people you consider to be your enemies—those who hurt you or hurt others. Do tonglen for them, thinking of them as having the same confusion and stuckness as your friend or yourself. Breathe in their pain and send them relief.

Tonglen can extend infinitely. As you do the practice, gradually over time your compassion naturally expands, and so does your realization that things are not as solid as you thought. As you do this practice, gradually at your own pace, you will be surprised to find yourself more and more able to be there for others even in what used to seem like impossible situations.

sixteen

servants
of peace

*What makes the paramitas different from ordinary actions
is that they are based on prajna. Prajna is a way of seeing
which continually dissolves any tendency to use things to
get ground under our feet, a kind of bullshit-detector that
protects us from becoming righteous.*

Suppose there were a place we could go to learn
the art of peace, a sort of boot camp for spiritual
warriors. Instead of spending hours and hours
disciplining ourselves to defeat the enemy, we could
spend hours and hours dissolving the causes of war.

Such a place might be called bodhisattva training—or
training for servants of peace. The word *bodhisattva* refers
to those who have committed themselves to the path of
compassion. The boot camp might be run by Nelson
Mandela, Mother Teresa, and His Holiness the Dalai
Lama. More likely it would be run by people we've never
seen or heard of, just ordinary men and women from all

over the world who devote their lives to helping others be free of pain.

The methods we learn at the bodhisattva training might include meditation practice and tonglen. They might also include the six *paramitas*—the six activities of the servants of peace.

The word *paramita* means "going to the other shore." These actions are like a raft that carries us across the river of samsara. The paramitas are also called transcendent actions because they are based on going beyond the conventional notions of virtue and nonvirtue. They train us in stepping beyond the limitations of dualistic views altogether and developing a flexible mind.

One of the main challenges of this camp would be to avoid becoming moralistic. With people coming from all nations, there would be many conflicting opinions about what was ethical and what was unethical, about what was helpful and what was not. Very soon we'd probably need to request the most tamed and awakened people there to lead a course on flexibility and humor!

In his own way, Trungpa Rinpoche devised such a course for his students. He'd have us memorize certain chants, and a few months after most of us knew them, he'd change the wording. He'd teach us specific rituals and be extremely precise about how they should be done. Just about the time we began criticizing people who did them wrong, he'd teach the rituals in a completely different way. We would print up nice manuals with all the correct procedures, but usually they were outdated before they came off the press. After years of this sort of training, one begins to relax one's grip. If today the instruction is to put everything on the right, one does that as impeccably as one can. When tomorrow the instruction is to put everything on the left, one does that with one's whole heart. The idea of one right way sort of dissolves into the mist.

Meditation and tonglen are well-tested methods for training in adaptability and letting go of rigid mind. The six paramitas complement these practices and bring the training into all the activities of our life. They become the means for making everything we do a way of living the art of peace.

What makes the paramitas different from ordinary actions is that they are based on *prajna*. Prajna is a way of seeing which continually dissolves any tendency to use things to get ground under our feet, a kind of bullshit-detector that protects us from becoming righteous.

When we are training in the art of peace, we are not given any promises that, because of our noble intentions, everything will be okay. In fact, there are no promises of fruition at all. Instead, we are encouraged to simply look deeply at joy and sorrow, at laughing and crying, at hoping and fearing, at all that lives and dies. We learn that what truly heals is gratitude and tenderness.

It isn't that we say, "It doesn't matter about me all that much, but if I changed the world, it would be better for other people." It's less complicated than that. We don't set out to save the world; we set out to wonder how other people are doing and to reflect on how our actions affect other people's hearts.

The first five transcendent actions are generosity, discipline, patience, exertion, and meditation. These are inseparable from the sixth—the prajna that makes it impossible to use our actions as ways of becoming secure. Prajna is the wisdom that cuts through the immense suffering that comes from seeking to protect our own territory.

The very words *generosity, discipline, patience*, and *exertion* may have rigid connotations for many of us. They may sound like a heavy list of "shoulds" and "shouldn'ts." They might remind us of school rules or the preaching of moralists. However, these paramitas are not about measuring up. If we think they are about achieving some standard of perfection, then we'll feel defeated before we even begin. It is more accurate to express the paramitas as a journey of exploration, not as commandments carved in rock.

The first paramita is generosity, the journey of learning how to give. When we feel inadequate and unworthy, we hoard things. We are so afraid—afraid of losing, afraid of feeling even more poverty-stricken than we do already. This stinginess is extremely sad. We could look into it and shed a tear that we grasp and cling so fearfully. This holding on causes us to suffer greatly. We wish for comfort, but instead we reinforce aversion, the sense of sin, and the feeling that we are a hopeless case.

The causes of aggression and fear begin to dissolve by themselves when we move past the poverty of holding back. So the basic idea of generosity is to train in thinking bigger, to do ourselves the world's biggest favor and stop cultivating our own scheme. The more we experience fundamental richness, the more we can loosen our grip.

This fundamental richness is available in each moment. The key is to relax: relax to a cloud in the sky, relax to a tiny bird with gray wings, relax to the sound of the telephone ringing. We can see the simplicity in things as they are. We can smell things, taste things, feel emotions, and have memories. When we are able to be there without saying, "I certainly agree with this," or "I definitely don't agree with that," but just be here very directly, then we find fundamental richness everywhere. It is not ours or theirs but is available always to everyone. In raindrops, in blood drops, in heartache and delight, this wealth is the nature of everything. It is like the sun in that it shines on everyone without discrimination. It is like a mirror in that it is willing to reflect anything without accepting or rejecting.

The journey of generosity is one of connecting with this wealth, cherishing it so profoundly that we are willing to begin to give away whatever blocks it. We give away our dark glasses, our long coats, our hoods, and our disguises. In short, we open ourselves and let ourselves be touched. This is called building confidence in all-pervasive richness. At the everyday, ordinary level, we experience it as flexibility and warmth.

When one takes a formal bodhisattva vow, one presents a gift to the teacher as a focal point of the ceremony.

The guidelines are to give something that's precious, something one finds difficult to part with. I once spent an entire day with a friend who was trying to decide what to give. As soon as he thought of something, his attachment for it would become intense. After a while, he was a nervous wreck. Just the thought of losing even one of his favorite belongings was more than he could bear. Later I mentioned the episode to a visiting teacher, and he said perhaps it was the opportunity for that man to develop compassion for himself and for all others caught in the misery of craving—for all others who just can't let go.

Giving material goods can help people. If food is needed and we can give it, we do that. If shelter is needed, or books or medicine are needed, and we can give them, we do that. As best we can, we can care for whoever needs our care. Nevertheless, the real transformation takes place when we let go of our attachment and give away what we think we can't. What we do on the outer level has the power to loosen up deep-rooted patterns of holding on to ourselves.

To the degree that we can give like this, we can communicate this ability to others. This is called giving the gift of fearlessness. When we touch the simplicity and goodness of things and realize that fundamentally we are not stuck in the mud, then we can share that relief with other people. We can make this journey together. We share what we have learned about taking down sunshades and unlocking armor, about being fearless enough to remove our masks.

We also can give the gift of dharma. To the degree that we can, we give meditation instruction. We tell people about tonglen. We introduce them to books and tapes, tell them of talks and practice sessions. We give people the tools for finding out for themselves what encourages us to loosen our grip, what encourages us to think bigger.

To dissolve the causes of aggression takes discipline, gentle yet precise discipline. Without the paramita of discipline, we simply don't have the support we need to evolve.

I remember the first retreat I led after *The Wisdom of No Escape* had been published. Most people came to the retreat because they were inspired by the notion of maitri that permeates that book. About the third day of the program, we were all sitting there meditating when one woman suddenly stood up, stretched a bit, and lay down on the floor. When I asked her about it later, she said, "Well, I felt so tired that I thought I'd be kind to myself and give myself a break." It was then that I realized I needed to talk about the magic of discipline and not being swayed by moods.

The first time I meditated with Trungpa Rinpoche's students was in 1972. He hadn't been in North America for long, and his scene, as we used to call it, was just beginning to evolve. In one corner of the room, a man had propped himself up on three round cushions, and every five or ten minutes they'd all come crashing down. Then he'd set up his cushions again and continue. Another student kept jumping up and running out of the room crying. She did that about five times in a one-hour sitting. When we began walking meditation, there were as many different, eccentric styles as there were people. One person would bend deeply at the knee and sort of float upward on each step; someone else was walking backward. The whole thing was totally entertaining and totally distracting. Not long after that, Rinpoche slowly began to introduce a standard meditation-room form, and things settled down considerably.

What we discipline is not our "badness" or our "wrongness." What we discipline is any form of potential escape from reality. In other words, discipline allows us to be right here and connect with the richness of the moment.

What makes this discipline free from severity is prajna. It's not the same as being told not to enjoy anything pleasurable or to control ourselves at any cost. Instead, this journey of discipline provides the encouragement that allows us to let go. It's a sort of undoing process that supports us in going against the grain of our painful habitual patterns.

At the outer level, we could think of discipline as a structure, like a thirty-minute meditation period or a two-hour class on the dharma. Probably the best example is the meditation technique. We sit down in a certain position and are as faithful to the technique as possible. We simply put light attention on the out-breath over and over through mood swings, through memories, through dramas and boredom. This simple repetitive process is like inviting that basic richness into our lives. So we follow the instruction just as centuries of meditators have done before.

Within this structure, we proceed with compassion. So on the inner level, the discipline is to return to gentleness, to honesty, to letting go. At the inner level, the discipline is to find the balance between not too tight and not too loose—between not too laid-back and not too rigid.

Discipline provides the support to slow down enough and be present enough so that we can live our lives without making a big mess. It provides the encouragement to step further into groundlessness.

The power of the paramita of patience is that it is the antidote to anger, a way to learn to love and care for whatever we meet on the path. By patience, we do not mean enduring—grin and bear it. In any situation, instead of reacting suddenly, we could chew it, smell it, look at it, and open ourselves to seeing what's there. The opposite of patience is aggression—the desire to jump and move, to push against our lives, to try to fill up space. The journey of patience involves relaxing, opening to what's happening, experiencing a sense of wonder.

A friend told me how, in her childhood, her grandmother, who was part Cherokee, took her and her brother on walks to see animals. Her grandmother said, "If you sit still, you'll see something. If you're very quiet, you'll hear something." She never used the word *patience*, but that is what they learned.

One of the ways to practice patience is to do tonglen.

135

When we want to make a sudden move, when we start to speed through life, when we feel we must have resolution, when someone yells at us and we feel insulted, we want to yell back or get even. We want to put out our poison. Instead, we can connect with basic human restlessness, basic human aggression, by practicing tonglen for all beings. Then we can send out a sense of space, which further slows things down. Sitting there, standing there, we can allow the space for the usual habitual thing *not* to happen. Our words and actions might be quite different because we allowed ourselves time to touch and taste and see the situation first.

Like the other paramitas, exertion has a journey quality, a process quality. When we begin to practice exertion, we see that sometimes we can do it and sometimes we can't. The question becomes, How do we connect with inspiration? How do we connect with the spark and joy that's available in every moment? Exertion is not like pushing ourselves. It's not a project to complete or a race we have to win. It's like waking up on a cold, snowy day in a mountain cabin ready to go for a walk but knowing that first you have to get out of bed and make a fire. You'd rather stay in that cozy bed, but you jump out and make the fire because the brightness of the day in front of you is bigger than staying in bed.

The more we connect with a bigger perspective, the more we connect with energetic joy. Exertion is touching in to our appetite for enlightenment. It allows us to act, to give, to work appreciatively with whatever comes our way. If we really knew how unhappy it was making this whole planet that we all try to avoid pain and seek pleasure—how that was making us so miserable and cutting us off from our basic heart and our basic intelligence—then we would practice meditation as if our hair were on fire. We would practice as if a big snake had just landed in our lap. There wouldn't be any question of thinking we had a lot of time and we could do this later.

Because of prajna, these actions become the means of shedding our defenses. Every time we give, every time we practice discipline, patience, or exertion, it's like putting down a heavy burden.

The paramita of meditation allows us to continue this journey. It is the basis for an enlightened society that is not based on winning and losing, loss and gain.

When we sit down to meditate, we can connect with something unconditional—a state of mind, a basic environment that does not grasp or reject anything. Meditation is probably the only activity that doesn't add anything to the picture. Everything is allowed to come and go without further embellishment. Meditation is a totally nonviolent, nonaggressive occupation. Not filling the space, allowing for the possibility of connecting with unconditional openness—this provides the basis for real change. You might say this is setting ourselves a task that is almost impossible. Maybe that is true. But on the other hand, the more we sit with this impossibility, the more we find it's always possible after all.

When we cling to thoughts and memories, we are

clinging to what cannot be grasped. When we touch these phantoms and let them go, we may discover a space, a break in the chatter, a glimpse of open sky. This is our birthright—the wisdom with which we were born, the vast unfolding display of primordial richness, primordial openness, primordial wisdom itself. All that is necessary then is to rest undistractedly in the immediate present, in this very instant in time. And if we become drawn away by thoughts, by longings, by hopes and fears, again and again we can return to this present moment. We are here. We are carried off as if by the wind, and as if by the wind, we are brought back. When one thought has ended and another has not begun, we can rest in that space. We train in returning to the unchanging heart of this very moment. All compassion and all inspiration come from that.

The sixth paramita is prajna, that which turns all actions into gold. It is said that the other five paramitas could give us reference points, but prajna cuts through the whole thing. Prajna makes us homeless; we have no place to dwell on anything. Because of this, we can finally relax. No more fighting. No more biting. No more taking sides.

Sometimes we feel tremendous longing for our old habits. When we work with generosity, we see our nostalgia for wanting to hold on. When we work with discipline, we see our nostalgia for wanting to zone out and not relate at all. As we work with patience, we discover our longing to speed. When we practice exertion, we realize our laziness. With meditation we see our endless discursiveness, our restlessness, and our attitude of "couldn't care less."

So we simply let that nostalgia be and know that all human beings are going to feel like that. There's a place for nostalgia, just as there's a place for everything on this path. Year after year, we just keep taking off our armor and stepping further into groundlessness.

This is the training of the bodhisattva, the training of the servants of peace. The world needs people who are trained like this—bodhisattva politicians, bodhisattva police, bodhisattva parents, bodhisattva bus drivers, bodhisattvas at the bank and the grocery store. In all levels of society we are needed. We are needed to transform our minds and actions for the sake of other people and for the future of the world.

seventeen

opinions

When we hold on to our opinions with aggression, no matter
how valid our cause, we are simply adding more aggression to
the planet, and violence and pain increase. Cultivating
nonaggression is cultivating peace.

O ne of the best practices for everyday living when
we don't have much time for meditation is to
notice our opinions. When we are doing sitting
meditation, part of the technique is to become aware of
our thoughts. Then, without judgment, without calling
them right or wrong, we simply acknowledge that we are
thinking. It's an exercise in nonaggression toward ourselves. It is also an exercise in bringing out our intelligence: seeing that we're just thinking, but with no
attached hope or fear, praise or blame. But when we sit
down to meditate, it's not always that ideal. Often, noticing that we are thinking, even if it's only for a quarter of a
second out of an hour of sitting, is accompanied by blame
or praise. It's good or it's bad. In any case, there's more
involved than just labeling it "thinking."

But after we've practiced meditation for a while, because we just sit alone with ourselves doing nothing but being aware of our out-breath and noticing our thoughts, our minds become stiller. Therefore, we begin to notice everything more. Whether we think we're noticing more or not, we really are. In meditation we allow a lot of space, and then we begin to see whatever comes up with increasing clarity, with increasing vividness. We notice that we're churning out thoughts all the time and that there are also gaps in all that chatter. We also notice our attitudes about what is going on. Then we begin to be attuned to our habitual patterns and see what we do and who we are at the level of holding ourselves together with opinions and ideas about things.

When we're not in meditation, we could begin to notice our opinions just as we notice that we're thinking when we're meditating. This is an extremely helpful practice, because we have a lot of opinions, and we tend to take them as truth. But actually they aren't truth. They are just our opinions. We have a lot of emotional backup for these opinions. They are often judgmental or critical; they're sometimes about how nice or perfect something is. In any case, we have a lot of opinions.

Opinions are opinions, nothing more or less. We can begin to notice them, and we can begin to label them as opinions, just as we label thoughts as thoughts. Just by this simple exercise we are introduced to the notion of egolessness. All ego really is, is our opinions, which we take to be solid, real, and the absolute truth about how things are. To have even a few seconds of doubt about the solidity and absolute truth of our own opinions, just to begin to see that we do have opinions, introduces us to the possibility of egolessness. We don't have to make these opinions go away, and we don't have to criticize ourselves for having them. We could just notice what we say to ourselves and see how so much of it is just our particular take on reality which may or may not be shared by other people.

We can just let those opinions go, and come back to the immediacy of our experience. We can come back to looking at someone's face in front of us, to tasting our coffee, to brushing our teeth, to whatever we might be doing. If we can see our opinions as opinions and even for a moment let them go, and then come back to the immediacy of our experience, we may discover that we are in a brand-new world, that we have new eyes and new ears.

When I talk about noticing opinions, I'm talking about noticing them as a simple way of beginning to pay attention to what we think and do and how much energy comes along with that. Then we can also begin to realize how solid we make things and how easy it is to get into a war in which we want our opinions to win and someone else's to lose. It is especially tempting to do this when we're engaged in social action.

Let's use the example of the ozone layer. We can rightly say that the thinning of the ozone layer is a scientific fact; it's not simply an opinion. But if the way we work with trying not to further harm the ozone layer is to solidify our opinion against those we feel are at fault, then nothing ever changes; negativity begets negativity. In other words, no matter how well documented or noble our cause is, it won't be helped by our feeling aggression toward the oppressors or those who are promoting the danger. Nothing will ever change through aggression.

You could say that not much changes through nonaggression either. However, nonaggression benefits the earth profoundly. The root cause of famine, starvation, and cruelty at the personal level is aggression. When we hold on to our opinions with aggression, no matter how valid our cause, we are simply adding more aggression to the planet, and violence and pain increase. Cultivating nonaggression is cultivating peace. The way to stop the war is to stop hating the enemy. It starts with seeing our opinions of ourselves and of others as simply our take on reality and not making them a reason to increase the negativity on the planet.

The key is to realize the difference between opinions and clear-seeing intelligence. Intelligence is like seeing thoughts as thinking, not having opinions about whether those thoughts are right or wrong. In the context of social action, we can see that what a government or corporation or individual is doing is clearly causing rivers to be polluted or people and animals to be harmed. We can take photographs of it; we can document it. We can see that suffering is real. That is because of our intelligence and because we don't let ourselves be swept away by opinions of good and evil or hope and fear.

It's up to us to sort out what is opinion and what is fact; then we can see intelligently. The more clearly we can see, the more powerful our speech and our actions will be. The less our speech and actions are clouded by opinion, the more they will communicate, not only to the people who are polluting the rivers, but also to those who are going to put pressure on the people who are polluting the rivers.

Just as the Buddha taught, it's important to see suffering as suffering. We are not talking about ignoring or keeping quiet. When we don't buy into our opinions and solidify the sense of enemy, we will accomplish something. If we don't get swept away by our outrage, then we will see the cause of suffering more clearly. That is how the cessation of suffering evolves.

This process requires enormous patience. It's important to remember, when we're out there nonaggressively working for reform, that, even if our particular issue doesn't get resolved, we are adding peace to the world. We have to do our best and at the same time give up all hope of fruition. One piece of advice that Don Juan gave to Carlos Casteneda was to do everything as if it were the only thing in the world that mattered, while all the time knowing that it doesn't matter at all. That attitude leads to more appreciation and less burnout, because we do the job wholeheartedly and we care. On the other hand, each day is a new day; we're not too future oriented. Although we are going in a direction, and the direction is to help diminish suffering, we have to realize that part of helping is keeping our clarity of mind, keeping our hearts and our minds open. When circumstances make us feel like closing our eyes and shutting our ears and making other people into the enemy, social action can be the most advanced practice. How to continue to speak and act without aggression is an enormous challenge. The way to start is to begin to notice our opinions.

There is nobody on the planet, neither those whom we see as the oppressed nor those whom we see as the oppressor, who doesn't have what it takes to wake up. We all need support and encouragement to be aware of what we think, what we say, and what we do. Notice your opinions. If you find yourself becoming aggressive about your opinions, notice that. If you find yourself being nonaggressive, notice that. Cultivating a mind that does not grasp at right and wrong, you will find a fresh state of being. The ultimate cessation of suffering comes from that. Finally, never give up on yourself. Then you will never give up on others. Wholeheartedly do what it takes to awaken your clear-seeing intelligence, but one day at a time, one moment at a time. If we live that way, we will benefit this earth.

eighteen

secret oral instructions

In that awkward, ambiguous moment is our own wisdom
mind. Right there in the uncertainty of everyday chaos is
our own wisdom mind.

S ometimes late at night or on a long walk with a
friend, we find ourselves discussing our ideas about
how to live and how to act and what is important
in life. If we're studying Buddhism and practicing meditation, we might talk of no-self and emptiness, of patience
and generosity, of loving-kindness and compassion. We
might have just read something or heard some teachings
that turned our usual way of seeing things upside down.
We feel that we've just reconnected with a truth we've
always known and that if we could just learn more about
it, our life would be delightful and rich. We tell our
friends of our longing to shed the huge burden we feel
we've always carried. We suddenly are excited and feel it's
possible. We tell our friend of our inspiration and how it
opens up our life. "It is possible," we say, "to enjoy the

very same things that usually get us down. We can delight in our job, delight in riding the subway, delight in shoveling snow and paying bills and washing dishes."

You may have noticed, however, that there is frequently an irritating, if not depressing, discrepancy between our ideas and good intentions and how we act when we are confronted with the nitty-gritty details of real life situations.

One afternoon I was riding a bus in San Francisco, reading a very touching article on human suffering and helping others. The idea of being generous and extending myself to those in need became so poignant that I started to cry. People were looking at me as the tears ran down my cheeks. I felt a great tenderness toward everyone, and a commitment to benefit others arose in me. As soon as I got home, feeling pretty exhausted after working all day, the phone rang, and it was someone asking if I could please help her out by taking her position as a meditation leader that night. I said, "No, sorry, I need to rest," and hung up.

It's not a matter of the right choice or the wrong choice, but simply that we are often presented with a dilemma about bringing together the inspiration of the teachings with what they mean to us on the spot. There is a perplexing tension between our aspirations and the reality of feeling tired, hungry, stressed-out, afraid, bored, angry, or whatever we experience in any given moment of our life.

Naropa, an eleventh-century Indian yogi, one day

unexpectedly met an old hag on the street. She apparently knew he was one of the greatest Buddhist scholars in India and asked him if he understood the words in the large book he was holding. He said he did, and she laughed and danced with glee. Then she asked him if he understood the meaning of the teachings in that book. Thinking to please her even more, he again said yes. At that point she became enraged, yelling at him that he was a hypocrite and a liar. That encounter changed Naropa's life. He knew she had his number: truthfully, he only understood the words and not the profound inner meaning of all the teachings he could expound so brilliantly.

This is where we also, to one degree or another, find ourselves. We can kid ourselves for a while that we understand meditation and the teachings, but at some point we have to face it. None of what we've learned seems very relevant when our lover leaves us, when our child has a tantrum in the supermarket, when we're insulted by our colleague. How do we work with our resentment when our boss walks into the room and yells at us? How do we reconcile that frustration and humiliation with our longing to be open and compassionate and not to harm ourselves or others? How do we mix our intention to be alert and gentle in meditation with the reality that we sit down and immediately fall asleep? What about when we sit down and spend the entire time thinking about how we crave someone or something we saw on the way to the meditation hall? Or we sit down and squirm the whole morning because our knees hurt and our back hurts and we're bored and fed up? Instead of calm, wakeful, and ego-less, we find ourselves getting more edgy, irritable, and solid.

This is an interesting place to find oneself. For the practitioner, this is an exceedingly important place.

When Naropa, seeking the meaning behind the words, set out to find a teacher, he continually found himself in this position of being squeezed. Intellectually he knew all about compassion, but when he came upon a filthy, lice-infested dog, he looked away. In the same vein, he knew all about nonattachment and not judging, but when his teacher asked him to do something he disapproved of, he refused.

We continually find ourselves in that squeeze. It's a place where we look for alternatives to just being there. It's an uncomfortable, embarrassing place, and it's often the place where people like ourselves give up. We liked meditation and the teachings when we felt inspired and in touch with ourselves and on the right path. But what about when it begins to feel like a burden, like we made the wrong choice and it's not living up to our expectations at all? The people we are meeting are not all that sane. In fact, they seem pretty confused. The way the place is run is not up to par. Even the teacher is questionable.

This place of the squeeze is the very point in our meditation and in our lives where we can really learn something. The point where we are not able to take it or leave it, where we are caught between a rock and a hard place, caught with both the upliftedness of our ideas and the rawness of what's happening in front of our eyes—that is indeed a very fruitful place.

When we feel squeezed, there's a tendency for mind to become small. We feel miserable, like a victim, like a pathetic, hopeless case. So believe it or not, at that moment of hassle or bewilderment or embarrassment, our minds could become bigger. Instead of taking what's occurred as a statement of personal weakness or someone else's power, instead of feeling we are stupid or someone else is unkind, we could drop all the complaints about ourselves and others. We could be there, feeling off guard, not knowing what to do, just hanging out there with the raw and tender energy of the moment. This is the place where we begin to learn the meaning behind the concepts and the words.

We're so used to running from discomfort, and we're so predictable. If we don't like it, we strike out at someone or beat up on ourselves. We want to have security and certainty of some kind when actually we have no ground to stand on at all.

The next time there's no ground to stand on, don't consider it an obstacle. Consider it a remarkable stroke of luck. We have no ground to stand on, and at the same time it could soften us and inspire us. Finally, after all these years, we could truly grow up. As Trungpa Rinpoche once said, the best mantra is "OM—grow up—*swaha*."

We are given changes all the time. We can either cling to security, or we can let ourselves feel exposed, as if we had just been born, as if we had just popped out into the brightness of life and were completely naked.

Maybe that sounds too uncomfortable or frightening, but on the other hand, it's our chance to realize that this mundane world is all there is, and we could see it with new eyes and at long last wake up from our ancient sleep of preconceptions.

The truth, said an ancient Chinese master, is neither like this nor like that. It is like a dog yearning over a bowl of burning oil. He can't leave it, because it is too desirable, and he can't lick it, because it is too hot.

So how do we relate to that squeeze? Somehow, someone finally needs to encourage us to be inquisitive about this unknown territory and about the unanswerable question of what's going to happen next.

The state of nowness is available in that moment of squeeze. In that awkward, ambiguous moment is our own wisdom mind. Right there in the uncertainty of everyday chaos is our own wisdom mind.

We need encouragement to experiment and try this kind of thing. It's quite daring, and maybe we feel we aren't up to it. But that's the point. Right there in that inadequate, restless feeling is our wisdom mind. We can simply experiment. There's absolutely nothing to lose. We could experiment with not getting tossed around by right and wrong and with learning to relax with groundlessness.

When I was a child, I had a picture book called *Lives of the Saints*. It was filled with stories of men and women who had never had an angry or mean thought and had never hurt a fly. I found the book totally useless as a guide for how we humans were supposed to live a good life. For me, *The Life of Milarepa* is a lot more instructive. Over the years, as I read and reread Milarepa's story, I find myself getting advice for where I am stuck and can't seem to move forward. To begin with, Milarepa was a murderer, and like most of us when we blow it, he wanted to atone for his errors. And like most of us, in the process of seeking liberation, he frequently fell flat on his face. He lied and stole to get what he wanted, he got so depressed he was suicidal, and he experienced nostalgia for the good old days. Like most of us, he had one person in his life who continually tested him and blew his saintly cover. Even when almost everyone regarded him as one of Tibet's most holy men, his vindictive old aunt continued to beat him with sticks and call him names, and he continued to have to figure out what to do with that kind of humiliating squeeze.

One can be grateful that a long lineage of teachers has worked with holding their seats with the big squeeze. They were tested and failed and still kept exploring how to just stay there, not seeking solid ground. They trained again and again throughout their lives not to give up on themselves and not to run away when the bottom fell out of their concepts and their noble ideals. From their own experience they have passed along to us the encouragement not to jump over the big squeeze, but to look at it just as it is, not just out of the corner of an eye. They showed us how to experience it fully, not as good or bad, but simply as unconditioned and ordinary.

This is the kind of instruction that Naropa received from his teacher Tilopa as he set out to find the profound meaning of all that occurs on the path. May we be as brave as he was in trying to find out what it means.

nineteen

three methods for working with chaos

The main point of these methods is to dissolve the
dualistic struggle, our habitual tendency to struggle
against what's happening to us or in us. These
methods instruct us to move toward difficulties
rather than backing away. We don't get this kind
of encouragement very often.

We practice to liberate ourselves from a burden—the burden of a narrow perspective
caused by craving, aggression, ignorance, and
fear. We're burdened by the people with whom we live,
by ongoing daily situations, and most of all by our own
personalities.

Through practice, we realize that we don't have to
obscure the joy and openness that is present in every
moment of our existence. We can awaken to basic goodness, our birthright. When we are able to do this, we no
longer feel burdened by depression, worry, or resentment.
Life feels spacious, like the sky and the sea. There's room

to relax and breathe and swim, to swim so far out that we no longer have the reference point of the shore.

How do we work with a sense of burden? How do we learn to relate with what seems to stand between us and the happiness we deserve? How do we learn to relax and connect with fundamental joy?

Times are difficult globally; awakening is no longer a luxury or an ideal. It's becoming critical. We don't need to add more depression, more discouragement, or more anger to what's already here. It's becoming essential that we learn how to relate sanely with difficult times. The earth seems to be beseeching us to connect with joy and discover our innermost essence. This is the best way that we can benefit others.

There are three traditional methods for relating directly with difficult circumstances as a path of awakening and joy. The first method we'll call no more struggle; the second, using poison as medicine; and the third, seeing whatever arises as enlightened wisdom. These are three techniques for working with chaos, difficulties, and unwanted events in our daily lives.

The first method, no more struggle, is epitomized by shamatha-vipashyana instruction. When we sit down to meditate, whatever arises in our minds we look at directly, call it "thinking," and go back to the simplicity and immediacy of the breath. Again and again, we return to pristine awareness free from concepts. Meditation practice is how we stop fighting with ourselves, how we stop struggling with circumstances, emotions, or moods. This basic instruction is a tool that we can use to train in our practice and in our lives. Whatever arises, we can look at it with a nonjudgmental attitude.

This instruction applies to working with unpleasantness in its myriad guises. Whatever or whoever arises, train again and again in looking at it and seeing it for what it is without calling it names, without hurling rocks, without averting your eyes. Let all those stories go. The innermost essence of mind is without bias. Things arise and things dissolve forever and ever. That's just the way it is.

This is the primary method for working with painful situations—global pain, domestic pain, any pain at all. We can stop struggling with what occurs and see its true face without calling it the enemy. It helps to remember that our practice is not about accomplishing anything—not about winning or losing—but about ceasing to struggle and relaxing as it is. That is what we are doing when we sit down to meditate. That attitude spreads into the rest of our lives.

It's like inviting what scares us to introduce itself and hang around for a while. As Milarepa sang to the monsters he found in his cave, "It is wonderful you demons came today. You must come again tomorrow. From time to time, we should converse." We start by working with the monsters in our mind. Then we develop the wisdom and compassion to communicate sanely with the threats and fears of our daily life.

The Tibetan yogini Machig Labdrön was one who fearlessly trained with this view. She said that in her tradition they did not exorcise demons. They treated them with compassion. The advice she was given by her teacher and passed on to her students was, "Approach what you find repulsive, help the ones you think you cannot help, and go to places that scare you." This begins when we sit down to meditate and practice not struggling with our own mind.

The second method of working with chaos is using poison as medicine. We can use difficult situations—poison—as fuel for waking up. In general, this idea is introduced to us with tonglen.

When anything difficult arises—any kind of conflict, any notion of unworthiness, anything that feels distasteful, embarrassing, or painful—instead of trying to get rid of it, we breathe it in. The three poisons are passion (this includes craving or addiction), aggression, and ignorance (which includes denial or the tendency to shut down and close out). We would usually think of these poisons as something bad, something to be avoided. But that isn't the attitude here; instead, they become seeds of compassion and openness. When suffering arises, the tonglen instruction is to let the story line go and breathe it in—not just the anger, resentment, or loneliness that we might be feeling, but the identical pain of others who in this very moment are also feeling rage, bitterness, or isolation.

We breathe it in for everybody. This poison is not just our personal misfortune, our fault, our blemish, our shame—it's part of the human condition. It's our kinship with all living things, the material we need in order to understand what it's like to stand in another person's shoes. Instead of pushing it away or running from it, we breathe in and connect with it fully. We do this with the wish that all of us could be free of suffering. Then we breathe out, sending out a sense of big space, a sense of ventilation or freshness. We do this with the wish that all of us could relax and experience the innermost essence of our mind.

We are told from childhood that something is wrong with us, with the world, and with everything that comes along: it's not perfect, it has rough edges, it has a bitter taste, it's too loud, too soft, too sharp, too wishy-washy. We cultivate a sense of trying to make things better because something is bad here, something is a mistake here, something is a problem here. The main point of these methods is to dissolve the dualistic struggle, our habitual tendency to struggle against what's happening to us or in us. These methods instruct us to move toward difficulties rather than backing away. We don't get this kind of encouragement very often.

Everything that occurs is not only usable and workable but is actually the path itself. We can use everything that happens to us as the means for waking up. We can use everything that occurs—whether it's our conflicting emotions and thoughts or our seemingly outer situation—to show us where we are asleep and how we can wake up completely, utterly, without reservations.

So the second method is to use poison as medicine, to use difficult situations to awaken our genuine caring for other people who, just like us, often find themselves in pain. As one lojong slogan says, "When the world is filled with evil, all mishaps, all difficulties, should be transformed into the path of enlightenment." That's the notion engendered here.

The third method for working with chaos is to regard whatever arises as the manifestation of awakened energy. We can regard ourselves as already awake; we can regard our world as already sacred. Traditionally the image used for regarding whatever arises as the very energy of wisdom is the charnel ground. In Tibet the charnel grounds were what we call graveyards, but they weren't quite as pretty as our graveyards. The bodies were not under a nice smooth lawn with little white stones carved with angels and pretty words. In Tibet the ground was frozen, so the bodies were chopped up after people died and taken to the charnel grounds, where the vultures would eat them. I'm sure the charnel grounds didn't smell very good and were alarming to see. There were eyeballs and hair and bones and other body parts all over the place. In a book about Tibet, I saw a photograph in which people were bringing a body to the charnel ground. There was a circle of vultures that looked to be about the size of two-year-old children—all just sitting there waiting for this body to arrive.

Perhaps the closest thing to a charnel ground in our world is not a graveyard but a hospital emergency room. That could be the image for our working basis, which is grounded in some honesty about how the human realm functions. It smells, it bleeds, it is full of unpredictability, but at the same time, it is self-radiant wisdom, good food, that which nourishes us, that which is beneficial and pure.

Regarding what arises as awakened energy reverses our fundamental habitual pattern of trying to avoid conflict, trying to make ourselves better than we are, trying to smooth things out and pretty them up, trying to prove that pain is a mistake and would not exist in our lives if only we did all the right things. This view turns that particular pattern completely around, encouraging us to become interested in looking at the charnel ground of our lives as the working basis for attaining enlightenment.

Often in our daily lives we panic. We feel heart palpitations and stomach rumblings because we are arguing with someone or because we had a beautiful plan and it's not working out. How do we walk into those dramas? How do we deal with those demons, which are basically our hopes and fears? How do we stop struggling against ourselves? Machig Labdrön advises that we go to places that scare us. But how do we do that?

We're trying to learn not to split ourselves between our "good side" and our "bad side," between our "pure side" and our "impure side." The elemental struggle is with our feeling of being wrong, with our guilt and shame at what we are. That's what we have to befriend. The point is that we can dissolve the sense of dualism between us and them, between this and that, between here and there, by moving toward what we find difficult and wish to push away.

161

In terms of everyday experience, these methods encourage us not to feel embarrassed about ourselves. There is nothing to be embarrassed about. It's like ethnic cooking. We could be proud to display our Jewish matzo balls, our Indian curry, our African American chitlins, our middle American hamburger and fries. There's a lot of juicy stuff we could be proud of. Chaos is part of our home ground. Instead of looking for something higher or purer, work with it just as it is.

The world we find ourselves in, the person we think we are—these are our working bases. This charnel ground called life is the manifestation of wisdom. This wisdom is the basis of freedom and also the basis of confusion. In every moment of time, we make a choice. Which way do we go? How do we relate to the raw material of our existence?

These are three very practical ways to work with chaos: no struggle, poison as medicine, and regarding everything that arises as the manifestation of wisdom. First, we can train in letting the story lines go. Slow down enough to just be present, let go of the multitude of judgments and schemes, and stop struggling. Second, we can use every day of our lives to take a different attitude toward suffering. Instead of pushing it away, we can breathe it in with the wish that everyone could stop hurting, with the wish that people everywhere could experience contentment in their hearts. We could transform pain into joy.

Third, we can acknowledge that suffering exists, that

darkness exists. The chaos in here and the chaos out there—this is basic energy, the play of wisdom. Whether we regard our situation as heaven or as hell depends on our perception.

Finally, couldn't we just relax and lighten up? When we wake up in the morning, we can dedicate our day to learning how to do this. We can cultivate a sense of humor and practice giving ourselves a break. Every time we sit down to meditate, we can think of it as training to lighten up, to have a sense of humor, to relax. As one student said, "Lower your standards and relax as it is."

twenty

the trick of choicelessness

We don't experience the world fully unless we are
willing to give everything away. Samaya means not
holding anything back, not preparing our escape
route, not looking for alternatives, not thinking
that there is ample time to do things later.

The teachings of Buddhism are directed at people
who don't have a lot of time to waste. That
includes all of us, whether we're aware of it or not.
From the point of view of the teachings, thinking that we
have ample time to do things later is the greatest myth,
the greatest hang-up, and the greatest poison. That, along
with our continual, deep-seated tendency to try to get
away from what we are doing, clouds our perceptions and
our thinking. If we knew that tonight we were going to go
blind, we would take a longing, last *real* look at every
blade of grass, every cloud formation, every speck of dust,
every rainbow, raindrop—everything. If we knew that we
were going to be deaf tomorrow, we would treasure every

single sound we heard. The teachings of the vajrayana*
try to scare us into waking up to how little time there is
and to the preciousness of human birth.

In the vajrayana, there is something called the *samaya*
bond, whereby the student's total experience is bound
to the path. At a certain time, after a lot of intelligent
questioning, the student may finally feel ready to enter
into a samaya relationship with his or her teacher. If the
student accepts and trusts the teacher completely and
the teacher accepts the student, they can enter into the
unconditional relationship called samaya. The teacher
will never give up on the student no matter how mixed
up he or she might be, and the student will also never
leave the teacher, no matter what.

The student and teacher are bound together. It's like a
pact that they make to attain enlightenment together.
Another definition of samaya is "sacred oath," or "sacred
commitment." But it's nothing holy; it's a commitment to
sanity—to indestructible sanity. Samaya is like a marriage
with reality, a marriage with the phenomenal world. But
it's a trick. This marriage is a little bit like having amnesia.
We think that we have decided to marry this partner of
our own free choice; however, unknown to us, we already
are married.

Samaya is a trick because we think we have a choice
about whether or not to make this commitment to sanity,
but the fact is, it's been choiceless all along. It's a compas-

* *The "diamond vehicle"; the practice of taking the results as the path.*

sionate trick, a trick to help us to realize that there really is
no exit. There really is no better time than right now; there
is no higher state of consciousness than this one. It's the
kind of trick that vajrayana teachers devise in their spare
time for their thorough, complete, and utter enjoyment:
"How can we trick these confused, bewildered, untamable
beings into realizing that they're already awake—and that
it's choiceless?"

From the point of view of samaya, we could say that
looking for alternatives is the only thing that keeps us from
realizing that we're already in a sacred world. Looking for
alternatives—better sights than we see, better sounds than
we hear, a better mind than we have—keeps us from realizing that we could stand with pride in the middle of our life
and realize it's a sacred mandala. We have such a deep tendency to want to squirm out of it, like a beetle on a pin: we
squirm and try to get away from just being on the dot.

In vajrayana Buddhism there are descriptions of many
different samayas, but they all have to do with realizing that
we are bound to reality already; they all trick us into that
choiceless situation. Even if every inch of our being wants
to run in the opposite direction, we stay here. There is
no other way to enter sacred world. We have to stop thinking that we can get away and settle down somewhere
else. Instead, we could just relax—relax with exhaustion,
indigestion, insomnia, irritation, delight, whatever.

The most important samayas are the samayas of body,
speech, and mind. First is being bound to body, bound to
form, to what we see with our eyes—sticking with that

and never giving up on what we see with our eyes.

It is said that the samayas of body, speech, and mind are as continuous as a river flowing. That's not our usual experience. Our usual experience is that, just when our perception is getting vivid, we get jumpy. The world is always displaying itself, always waving and winking, but we are so self-involved that we miss it. The experience of sticking with it, of not giving up, is one in which the whole world, everything that we see, becomes extremely vivid and more solid, and at the same time, less substantial and more transparent. We're not talking about seeing anything other than the person sitting in front of us: seeing how his or her hair sticks up or lies down, is dirty or clean, brushed or gnarled; or seeing a bird with black feathers and a twig in its mouth, sitting in a tree. The things we see all the time can pop us out of the painful cycle of samsara.

If we stick with it, our experience becomes more vivid and more transparent, and we can no longer *not* get the message. And this is a message that never gets interpreted. Things speak for themselves. It's not that red cushion means passion, or little mouse darting in and out means discursive mind; it's just red cushion and little mouse peeping out from behind the chair.

Sound is the same thing, ordinary sound—every sound that we ever hear, from the alarm clock waking us up in the morning to our snoring companion at night. We all know what sounds are like when they punctuate and startle us, but what does your pen sound like, writing in your notebook? And how does it sound when you turn the pages of this book? What about your own voice? It's interesting to hear one's own voice; it sounds like someone else's voice. To hear what we say and see how it goes out into the environment and communicates also has the power to pop us out of the deadness of samsara. Even if we're alone, our yawns and farts communicate. So every ordinary little peep or scratch or snicker, every little chewing sound or drinking sound or whatever, can wake us up. The idea of samaya is that if we don't avoid our personal experience—if we don't think there's a better, more inspiring, less irritating, or less disturbing sound—sounds become vivid and transparent.

The same goes for mind. As we practice, we see that thoughts do not go away; they become more precise and less substantial. At the level of mind, we break samaya by making things "wrong" or making things "right." We think we have some choice to make, some alternative to just hanging out with not solving anything, not resolving anything. We could say that, at the level of mind, breaking samaya is feeling that we must come up with a solution to a problem—or feeling that there is a solution or a problem at all. That might give you some idea of how difficult it is to keep samaya.

Traditionally it is said that keeping the samaya bond is like keeping a mirror polished: As soon as it has been cleaned, dust begins to alight. The samaya bond is experiential and can be violated by a moment of distraction. Nevertheless, we can mend it instantly by following the same familiar instruction of just coming back to this very moment.

Trungpa Rinpoche's *Sadhana of Mahamudra* describes the samaya of body, speech, and mind in a beautiful way: "Whatever is seen with the eyes is vividly unreal in emptiness, yet there is still form." It goes on to say that this is none other than the appearance of our teacher. "Whatever is heard with the ears is the echo of emptiness, yet real." And these ordinary, everyday sounds are the utterance of our teacher. All our thoughts and memories, "good and bad, happy and sad," all "vanish into emptiness like the imprint of a bird in the sky." All these constantly arising thoughts are the mind of our teacher. This is where we begin to be introduced to the fact that our teacher is not separate from our experience. We realize that there is no alternative to the experience that we have. Our experience is the only experience there is. This is the ultimate teacher.

According to a famous quote, the student of vajrayana Buddhism should always be in a state of panic. It is so unfamiliar to us to make such a total commitment to being awake that it unnerves us. Once when I was spending hours and hours doing a certain practice, I became so agitated that I could hardly sit still. Later, I told Rinpoche that I felt irritated at *everything*, even little specks of dust. He said that happened because the practice was demanding me to be sane and I wasn't used to that yet.

In the case of samaya, when we talk about commitment, it's total commitment: total commitment to sanity, total commitment to our experience, an unconditional relationship with reality. People always say that that's what they want: they want someone to love them unconditionally, and they want to love someone unconditionally. We think we'd be delighted to have an unconditional relationship, but that's only as long as it's on our own terms. Anyone who has been married or in a long-term relationship knows that challenges present themselves. The challenges are to give in, to surrender our way of doing things, and not to split when we feel threatened. Basically, the challenge is to be genuine—to feel our pounding heart or shaking knees or whatever it is, and stick with it. In a nutshell, very few of us ever allow ourselves to be in a situation that doesn't have at least a teensy-weensy little exit, a place where we can get out if we have to.

In the sixties in New Mexico, I used to go to sweat lodges. I would insist on sitting by the door, because if I was anywhere but by the door, I couldn't get out. It would get hotter and hotter and hotter in there, and the steam would fill the space, and I was sure I was going to die. But if I could sit by the door and *know* that I could leave, then I could make it through. Of course, if I sat away from the door, I *had* to make it through, but I would be so freaked out the whole time that it wasn't much fun. Well, with samaya, we do not get to sit by the door. It's the ultimate trick. It's the only way we finally experience our experience; it's our only entrance into the self-existing sacredness of the world.

Before we feel ready for this kind of demand, we make

a journey. We start with our confusion and our wildness, and we begin to let meditation and the teachings tame us. We take what we hear to heart, and we do our best to put it into practice in our everyday life. This sincere effort begins to calm us down. It isn't that suddenly we become perfect and sit far away from the door. It's more that through years and years of gentle training and honest, intelligent inquiry, we begin to trust our basic wisdom mind. We find that we have an essential wisdom, an essential good heart, that is stronger and more fundamental than our unkindness and aggression. As we practice, we uncover that wisdom. It's like finding that the sky and the sun are always there and that it's the storms and clouds that come and go. Somehow, feeling that we are ready to have no exit just occurs by itself.

Naropa's foremost student was a Tibetan named Marpa the Translator. On one of his trips to India, Marpa had collected the traditional gold to give to the teacher. Now Marpa was not exactly a coward, and he was not exactly stingy; he was a very bold, gutsy kind of fellow. For instance, his friends and family tried to get someone to walk with him from Tibet to India, and he refused to have company, even though his health wasn't all that good and he was over fifty years old.

So the story goes that Marpa made his final gift of gold to his teacher Naropa, but he kept a *little* back—just as we always do. And there was a reasonable explanation for this: he had to travel home, and he needed a little gold— just a little. But Naropa said, "Do you think you can buy me with your deception?" So Marpa gave him all of it. Naropa threw the gold up into the air and said, "The whole world is gold to me." At that point Marpa realized the nature of reality more vividly than ever before.

We don't experience the world fully unless we are willing to give everything away. Samaya means not holding anything back, not preparing our escape route, not looking for alternatives, not thinking that there is ample time to do things later.

In some sense, the whole samaya relationship— whether it's with the phenomenal world as absolute teacher or with an individual person—is about softening us up. It softens us up so that we can't deceive ourselves; so that we can't be deaf, dumb, and blind; so that we always get the message. The samaya relationship with a vajrayana teacher is meant to help us: it's meant to introduce us to the fact that if we could have an unconditional relationship with even one person, we could have an unconditional relationship with the world. Up to that point, we think that we can get away, that we can squirm out of it. But in this particular relationship, we make a commitment to hang in there no matter what happens.

Marpa's principal student was Milarepa, and initially their relationship was a tough one. Milarepa had no doubt that Marpa was his teacher and that Marpa could lead him to enlightenment. Therefore, Milarepa told him, "I commit myself to you totally with body, speech, and mind. Please help me to realize my true nature." Then the challenges began. Milarepa had accumulated a lot of karmic baggage. In particular, he had killed a lot of people and caused a lot of pain. In order for him to put down that load, he had to undergo many trials. Marpa kept making him build towers; when they were almost complete, he would yell at Milarepa to tear them down. Milarepa suffered much in his early years with Marpa. He couldn't get any teachings, and he was continually insulted, and he built towers until his hands and back were one big sore. Nevertheless, Milarepa never doubted Marpa's motivation, and in truth, although he rarely displayed it, Marpa loved Milarepa with his whole heart and wanted only to help him wake up fully. Each time Milarepa surrendered to the situation, each time he dropped his resentment, depression, and pride, he was dropping his ancient habitual baggage. At a certain point, he was so naked that he had nothing left to lose. Then Marpa gave him the teachings and their relationship entered a new phase of tenderness and warmth.

But it's a process. In the beginning, our habit of running away is so deep-seated that we just experiment with this trick of being bound. We do this by practicing meditation. At first the meditation instruction is all we have to keep us from dissociating from our body, speech, and mind. Year after year, we just keep practicing coming back to our own experience of being in the present moment.

Making a formal samaya bond and entering into an unconditional relationship with a teacher is like putting ourselves in the jaws of a crocodile. We need to take a long time to decide we trust that particular crocodile enough to stick with him or her no matter what.

My own experience of this process was very gradual. When I first met Trungpa Rinpoche, I thought, "Now here is someone I cannot con." That was why I moved to Colorado, where I could spend more time in his presence. I moved closer, but I was definitely not ready to surrender.

There was intelligence in this: Rinpoche often scared me and outraged me. I wasn't sure I could trust him, and most important, I wasn't sure I loved him. In fact, I remember a whole retreat during which I would look at his picture and cry because I couldn't feel what I thought was proper devotion.

At the same time, I kept moving closer. He was the only person I could talk to about where I felt stuck and where I felt open. He was the only person who could cut through all my trips. Every so often he'd suddenly speak to me—maybe in a crowd, maybe during a business meeting, always when I least expected it. He'd ask me a question or make a comment that would totally stop my mind.

Long after I became his student, and long after I began vajrayana practice—long after practitioners usually take the formal samaya vow with their teacher—I finally knew without any doubt that I could trust him with my life; no matter what he said or did, he was my link with sacred world. Without him I wouldn't have a clue as to what that meant. It simply evolved that as I followed his teachings and woke up further, I finally realized his limitless kindness and experienced the vastness of his mind. At that point, the only place I wanted to be was in the jaws of the crocodile.

When I say that samaya is a trick, I mean that it tricks us into realizing that our relationship with the phenomenal world has always been choiceless. We don't really have a choice. The choice that we *think* we have is called ego. This choice that we think we have is what's keeping us from realizing that we're in sacred world; this choice that we think we have is like blinders, earplugs, and noseplugs. We are thoroughly conditioned so that the minute the seat gets hot, or we even think it's going to get hot, we jump off. The trick is to sit on the hot seat and have a commitment to our experience of hot-seatness. With or without a formal samaya with a teacher, this remains the main point.

To what do we really commit ourselves? Is it to playing it safe and manipulating our life and our whole world, so that it will give us security and confirmation? Or is our commitment to deeper and deeper levels of maitri? The question always remains: In what do we take refuge? Do we take refuge in small, self-satisfied actions, speech, and mind? Or do we take refuge in warriorship, in taking a leap, in going beyond our usual safety zones?

twenty-one

reversing the wheel
of samsara

Usually we feel that there's a large problem and we
have to fix it. The instruction is to stop. Do something
unfamiliar. Do anything besides rushing off in the same
old direction, up to the same old tricks.

S
omehow we keep distancing ourselves from the
dharma. It's as if we regard it as philosophy or a
crash course in self improvement, and no matter
how often we are encouraged to make meditation and the
teachings relevant to our emotional life, we continue to
forget to apply it when we get stuck. When we are angry
with someone or broken-hearted, when we want to get
even or commit suicide, at times like these we don't
seem to think meditation or the teachings quite cut
the mustard. They don't quite speak to the realness of the
situation.

Many people say that meditation is not enough, that
we need therapy and support groups to deal with our
most stuck patterns. They feel strongly that the dharma

doesn't quite penetrate our confusion deeply enough.

I often suggest therapy for a student. I see it as a specific skillful means that for some people is extremely helpful. For some of us, working closely with a nonjudgmental therapist allows us to overcome our fears and finally develop loving kindness for ourselves. At the same time, I know that not only is the dharma more revolutionary, but also that for many of us, the dharma itself supplies the tools and support we need to find our own beauty, our own insight, our own ability to work with neurosis and pain. One of the tricks seems to be having enough faith in the dharma to bring it right into our nightmares, not as an unusable theory that distances us from our major issues or something we're meant to measure up to, but as good food, no-side-effects medicine that is applicable always and everywhere.

The key is changing our habits and, in particular, the habits of our mind. I remember the day I understood without question that we create our situation by how we use our mind, by how we keep patterning our responses to life in the same old, very dusty, utterly predictable way. A situation came up about money. We were running out of money. I began to get tense. I felt as if a huge weight were literally sitting on my head. I began to panic. I had to find a way out. Until I found a way to solve this problem, I could not relax. I couldn't enjoy the sunshine on the water or the eagle sitting in a tree right outside my window.

The whole thing was hauntingly familiar. Why I

caught it this time more dramatically than ever before, I don't know. Probably it was a result of all the years of looking as honestly and uncritically as I could at my experience. Possibly it was also a result of all the meditation training I had done in seeing when I'd spin off and then just coming back to the present.

At any rate, that day I caught it. Right there in the middle of a very habitual state of mind, I saw what I was doing. I not only saw what I was doing, I also stopped. I stopped following through with my habitual plan to save the day. I decided not to rush around trying to avert disaster. I let the thoughts that "only I could rescue us" come and I let them go. I decided to see what would happen without my input—even if it meant that everything would fall apart. Sometimes you just have to let everything fall apart.

Stopping my actions was the first step and the hardest one. Not saving the day was going against the grain of how I operated. I felt like there was a huge wheel that had colossal momentum for going in a habitual direction, and I was turning it around.

That's what the dharma is about; turning all our habits around, reversing the process of how we make everything so solid, reversing the wheel of samsara. It starts with catching ourselves when we spin off in the same old ways. Usually we feel that there's a large problem and we have to fix it. The instruction is to stop. Do something unfamiliar. Do anything besides rushing off in the same old direction, up to the same old tricks.

In the Buddhist teachings, there is a lot of instruction for turning reality around. One hears advice like "Meditate on whatever provokes resentment" and "Lean into the sharp points." While Trungpa Rinpoche was still in Tibet, his teacher Khenpo Gangshar trained him in this style of living. He called it instruction in the nondual nature of reality. When we asked Rinpoche once what had happened to Khenpo Gangshar when they escaped from Tibet, he said he wasn't sure but had heard that when the rest of them were escaping to India, Khenpo Gangshar was walking toward China.

This kind of instruction is something we can apply to our lives, and it can bring about revolutionary changes in how we perceive things.

My first step was to decide I wasn't going to *act* on my habitual momentum. It was a test, an exploration of the Buddhist teaching that says we create our own reality, that what we perceive is our own projection.

Everything in me was dying to do the same old thing. But I kept remembering the teachings that say that until we stop clinging to the concept of good and evil, the world will continue to manifest as friendly goddesses and harmful demons. I wanted to explore whether this was true or not.

I could experiment this way without becoming rigid or harsh because of the training I'd had in making friends with my thoughts and emotions. Somehow, without cultivating unlimited friendliness for ourselves, we don't progress along the path. When we meditate and when we hear the teachings, it helps to remember that we are engaged in developing kindness.

One time when I was teaching in Austin, Texas, a man came up to me after the weekend and told me how much he appreciated the instruction to notice our tone of voice when we label our thoughts "thinking" and, if it's harsh, to say it again with gentleness. "I really took that to heart," he said, "and now when my mind wanders off, I just say to myself, 'Thinkin', good buddy.' "

Still, even after many years, many of us continue to practice harshly. We practice with guilt, as if we're going to be excommunicated if we don't do it right. We practice so we won't be ashamed of ourselves and with fear that someone will discover what a "bad" meditator we really are. The old joke is that a Buddhist is someone who is either meditating or feeling guilty about not meditating. There's not much joy in that.

Maybe the most important teaching is to lighten up and relax. It's such a huge help in working with our crazy mixed up minds to remember that what we're doing is unlocking a softness that is in us and letting it spread. We're letting it blur the sharp corners of self-criticism and complaint.

Some of us can accept others right where they are a lot more easily than we can accept ourselves. We feel that compassion is reserved for someone else, and it never occurs to us to feel it for ourselves.

My experience is that by practicing without "shoulds," we gradually discover our wakefulness and our confidence.

Gradually, without any agenda except to be honest and kind, we assume responsibility for being here in this unpredictable world, in this unique moment, in this precious human body.

Finally I came to that moment when I was ready to slow down the habitual momentum of my mind and stop being so predictable. I began with not acting in the familiar way. It felt difficult. There was such a huge longing to solve the problem, what Trungpa Rinpoche called "nostalgia for samsara." But my curiosity about the teachings was stronger than the yearning to do what I'd always done. Here I was stepping into no–man's–land. Here I was feeling shaky. It was real, not some lofty theory I'd read in a book. I didn't know what would happen next, but anything was preferable to reacting in the same stuck way.

Every act counts. Every thought and emotion counts too. This is all the path we have. This is where we apply the teachings. This is where we come to understand why we meditate. We are only going to be here for a short while. Even if we live to be 108, our life will be too short for witnessing all its wonders. The dharma is each act, each thought, each word we speak. Are we at least willing to catch ourselves spinning off and to do that without embarrassment? Do we at least aspire to not consider ourselves a problem, but simply a pretty typical human being who could at that moment give him- or herself a break and stop being so predictable?

My experience is that this is how our thoughts begin to slow down. Magically, it seems that there's a lot more space to breathe, a lot more room to dance, and a lot more happiness.

The dharma can heal our wounds, our very ancient wounds that come not from original sin but from a misunderstanding so old that we can no longer see it. The instruction is to relate compassionately with where we find ourselves and to begin to see our predicament as workable. We are stuck in patterns of grasping and fixating which cause the same thoughts and reactions to occur again and again and again. In this way we project our world. When we see that, even if it's only for one second every three weeks, then we'll naturally discover the knack of reversing this process of making things solid, the knack of stopping the claustrophobic world as we know it, putting down our centuries of baggage, and stepping into new territory.

If you ask how in the world we can do this, the answer is simple. Make the dharma personal, explore it whole-heartedly, and relax.

twenty-two

the path is the goal

If there's any possibility for enlightenment, it's right now,
not at some future time. Now is the time.

What does it take to use the life we already have
in order to make us wiser rather than more
stuck? What is the source of wisdom, at a
personal, individual level?

To the degree that I've understood the teachings, the
answer to these questions seems to have to do with
bringing everything that we encounter to the path. Everything naturally has a ground, path, and fruition. This is
like saying that everything has a beginning, a middle, and
an end. But it is also said that the path itself is both the
ground and the fruition. So one sometimes reads, "The
path is the goal."

This path has one very distinct characteristic: it is not
prefabricated. It doesn't already exist. The path that we're
talking about is the moment-by-moment evolution of our
experience, the moment-by-moment evolution of the
world of phenomena, the moment-by-moment evolution
of our thoughts and our emotions.

The path is not Route 66—destination, Los Angeles. It's not as if we can take out a map and figure that this year we might make it to Gallup, New Mexico, and maybe by 2001, we'll be in L.A. The path is uncharted. It comes into existence moment by moment and at the same time drops away behind us. It's like riding in a train sitting backwards. We can't see where we're headed, only where we've been.

This is a very encouraging teaching, because it says that the source of wisdom is whatever is going to happen to us today. The source of wisdom is whatever is happening to us right at this very instant.

We're always in some kind of mood. It might be sadness, it might be anger, it might be not much of anything, just a kind of blur. It might be humor or contentment. In any case, whatever it is, that's the path.

When something hurts in life, we don't usually think of it as our path or as the source of wisdom. In fact, we think that the reason we're on the path is to get rid of this painful feeling. ("When I get to L.A., I won't feel this way anymore.") At that level of wanting to get rid of our feeling, we naively cultivate a subtle aggression against ourselves.

However, the fact is that anyone who has used the moments and days and years of his or her life to become wiser, kinder, and more at home in the world has learned from what has happened right now. We can aspire to be kind right in the moment, to relax and open our heart and mind to what is in front of us right in the moment.

Now is the time. If there's any possibility for enlightenment, it's right now, not at some future time. Now is the time.

Now is the only time. How we relate to it creates the future. In other words, if we're going to be more cheerful in the future, it's because of our aspiration and exertion to be cheerful in the present. What we do accumulates; the future is the result of what we do right now.

When we find ourselves in a mess, we don't have to feel guilty about it. Instead, we could reflect on the fact that how we relate to this mess will be sowing the seeds of how we will relate to whatever happens next. We can make ourselves miserable, or we can make ourselves strong. The amount of effort is the same. Right now we are creating our state of mind for tomorrow, not to mention this afternoon, next week, next year, and all the years of our lives.

Sometimes we meet someone who seems to have a great sense of well-being, and we wonder how that person got that way. We would like to be that way. That well-being is often a result of having been brave enough to be fully alive and awake to every moment of life, including all the lack of cheer, all the dark times, all the times when the clouds cover the sun. Through our own good spirit, we can be willing to relate directly with what's happening, with precision and gentleness. That's what creates fundamental cheerfulness, fundamental relaxation.

When we realize that the path is the goal, there's a sense of workability. Trungpa Rinpoche said, "Whatever occurs in the confused mind is regarded as the path. Everything is workable. It is a fearless proclamation, the lion's roar." Everything that occurs in our confused mind we can regard as the path. Everything is workable.

If we find ourselves in what seems like a rotten or painful situation and we think, "Well, how is *this* enlightenment?" we can just remember this notion of the path, that what seems undesirable in our lives doesn't have to put us to sleep. What seems undesirable in our lives doesn't have to trigger habitual reactions. We can let it show us where we're at and let it remind us that the teachings encourage precision and gentleness, with loving-kindness toward every moment. When we live this way, we feel frequently—maybe continuously—at a crossroads, never knowing what's ahead.

It's an insecure way to live. We often find ourselves in the middle of a dilemma—what should I do about the fact that somebody is angry with me? What should I do about the fact that I'm angry with somebody? Basically, the instruction is not to try to solve the problem but instead to use it as a question about how to let this very situation wake us up further rather than lull us into ignorance. We can use a difficult situation to encourage ourselves to take a leap, to step out into that ambiguity.

This teaching applies to even the most horrendous situations life can dish out. Jean-Paul Sartre said that there are two ways to go to the gas chamber, free or not free. This is our choice in every moment. Do we relate to our circumstances with bitterness or with openness?

That is why it can be said that whatever occurs can be regarded as the path and that all things, not just some things, are workable. This teaching is a fearless proclamation of what's possible for ordinary people like you and me.

We live in difficult times. One senses the strong possibility that conditions may become even worse. Trungpa Rinpoche passed on many teachings that relate to uplifting society. He passionately and fearlessly imparted instructions that could bring about an era of courage in which people could experience their goodness and extend themselves to others. To the extent that I have understood this heart advice, I now pass some of it on to you. May these teachings take root and flourish for the benefit of all sentient beings now and in the future.

bibliography

Lhalungpa, Lobsang P., trans. *The Life of Milarepa*. Boulder and London: Shambhala Publications, 1984.

Nalanda Translation Committee under the direction of Chögyam Trungpa, trans. *The Life of Marpa the Translator*. Boston and London: Shambhala Publications, 1986.

Trungpa, Chögyam. *Crazy Wisdom*. Boston and London: Shambhala Publications, 1991.

—*Cutting Through Spiritual Materialism*. Berkeley, Calif.: Shambhala Publications, 1973.

—*The Heart of the Buddha*. Boston and London: Shambhala Publications, 1991.

—*Shambhala: The Sacred Path of the Warrior*. Boulder and London: Shambhala Publications, 1984.

resources

For further information regarding meditation or inquiries about a dharma center near you, please contact one of the following centers.

Karmê Chöling
RR I, Box 3
Barnet, VT 05821
(802) 633-2384

Shambhala Europe
Wilhelmstrasse 20
Marburg, D-35037
Germany
(49.6421) 17020

Gampo Abbey
Pleasant Bay
Cape Breton, N.S. BOE 2PO, Canada
(902) 224-2752

Rocky Mountain Shambhala Center
4921 County Road 68C
Red Feather Lakes, CO 80545
(303) 881-2184

Shambhala International
1084 Tower Road, Halifax,
N.S. B3H 2Y5, Canada
(902) 425-4275

For information about Buddhist postsecondary
education, call or write:

The Naropa Institute
2130 Arapahoe Ave.
Boulder, CO 80302
(303) 444-0202

Audio tapes of talks by Pema Chödrön are
available from:

L. Van de Bunte
4040 Greenleaf Circle #310
Kalamazoo, MI 49008

Sounds True
735 Walnut St.
Boulder, CO 80302
(800) 333-9185

the places that scare you

pema chödrön

a guide to fearlessness

One of the most inspiring spiritual teachers of our time offers simple, practical advice for living with less fear, less anxiety and a more open heart.

We always have a choice, Pema Chödrön teaches: we can let the circumstances of our lives harden us and make us increasingly resentful and afraid, or we can let them soften us and make us kind.

This book shows us how to awaken our basic goodness and connect to others. In her lively, contemporary voice, Chödrön translates the wisdom of the Tibetan Buddhist tradition for the layperson. Her fans come from all religions and none. Her wisdom cuts across all traditions and religions – appealing to everyone from the Dalai Lama's followers to ordinary people trying to make sense of their lives. Particularly in these difficult times, this advice strikes just the right note, offering us comfort and challenging us to live deeply and contribute to creating a more loving world.

the wisdom of no escape

pema chödrön

how to love yourself and your world

This book is about saying yes to life in all its manifestations – embracing the potent mixture of joy, suffering,
brilliance and confusion that characterizes the human
experience. It exhorts us to wake up wholeheartedly to
everything and to use the abundant, richly textured fabric
of everyday life as our primary spiritual teacher and
guide. Pema Chödrön shows us the profound value of our
situation of 'no escape' from the ups and downs of life.

start where you are

pema chödrön

a guide to compassionate living

Start Where You Are is an indispensable handbook for cultivating fearlessness and awakening a compassionate heart. With insight and humour, Chödrön presents down-to-earth guidance on how to make friends with ourselves and develop genuine compassion towards others.

This book shows how we can 'start where we are' by embracing rather than denying the painful aspects of our lives. Pema Chödrön frames her teachings on compassion around fifty-nine traditional Tibetan Buddhist maxims, or slogans, such as: 'Always apply a joyful state of mind' and 'Be grateful to everyone'. Working with these slogans and through the practice of meditation, Start Where You Are shows how we can all develop the courage to work with our own inner pain and discover joy, well-being and confidence.